LIGHT FOR LIFE

Part One
The Mystery Believed

God With Us Publications

Catechesis is a work of the Church, a sharing in the teaching mission of the Body of Christ. Catechetical material, like iconography or liturgical chant, strives to speak of the Tradition of the Church. The individual's insights, perceptions, and experiences become significant in that they personalize this Tradition and give witness to it in our contemporary world.

Accordingly, each text is the work of those Byzantine Catholic Churches in North America which participate in ECDD, the catechetical arm of the bishops of Eastern Catholic Associates. Contributors to this text include Father David Petras, principal contributor, with Father Fred Saato and Deacon Kent Plowman of the Ruthenian and Melkite Greek Catholic jurisdictions respectively. The text was subsequently reviewed and approved by all the hierarchs of the thirteen participating dioceses, their directors of religious education and diocesan catechetical staffs. It therefore represents their communities' common faith and vision.

Iconographic drawings: Rev. Mark Melone
Cover design: Beverly Stoller, Studio of the Theotokos
Technical assistance: Joanna Dailey

GOD WITH US PUBLICATIONS
P.O. Box 99203
Pittsburgh, PA 15233

Printed in the U.S.A.

ISBN 1-887158-07-3 (Part One)
ISBN 1-887158-06-5 (Three Part Set)

Table of Contents

Acknowledgements

The versions of Scripture traditionally used in Byzantine Churches have been the Septuagint version of the Old Testament (LXX) and the "received text" of the New Testament. Whenever necessary, these readings have been translated for this work. Otherwise, sources for Scriptural citations are:

JB — *The Jerusalem Bible*, copyright 1966, Darton, Longman & Todd, Ltd.

NAB — *The New American Bible*, copyright 1970, the Confraternity of Christian Doctrine

RSV — *The Revised Standard Version,* copyright 1971, Division of Christian Education, National Council of Churches of Christ

TEV — *Today's English Version*, copyright 1966, American Bible Society

When references to the LXX and the Hebrew text differ, as in the numbering of the psalms, the LXX citation is given first.

Whenever possible, liturgical texts have been cited from versions in use among the Byzantine Catholic jurisdictions in North America.

About the Cover - In the Byzantine tradition, the MYSTERY BELIEVED is epitomized, not so much by a text, as by the life-giving cross of the Lord. The sign of the cross, made so often in liturgical and private prayer, is a non-verbal proclamation of faith in the heart of the Christian mystery: the Trinity, the incarnation and the saving death of Christ, which cannot be separated from His resurrection. This life-giving quality of the cross is represented, in this detail from an icon of the Exaltation of the Holy Cross, by the sprig of basil which St. Macarios carries along with the cross.

Prologue

"I have come so that they may have life, and have it to the full" (Jn 10:10 *JB*). With these words St. John's Gospel explains the purpose of the incarnation. The Word of God — who brought all things into being at creation (cf Jn 1:1-4) — now brings about a new creation by taking flesh to bring us life in its truest sense. The One who first gave us being now calls us beyond the confines of created time and space to a destiny-filled experience of His presence. Remade in the depths of our being through this encounter, the Christian faithful of our day echo the cry of the first believers, "From his fulness we have, all of us, received — yes, grace upon grace" (Jn 1:16 *JB* alt).

The recreating presence of the Word of God among us opens the way for us to share in the "grace" of God: not an object or thing, but the very fullness of God Himself graciously given to us. Through Christ we are offered an entry into the intimate life of God and the mystery of the Holy Trinity. And it is *faith*, that openness to the working of God both in the world and in the depths of our being, which frees each of us to partake of this newness of life. It is, the Scripture says, "... to all who received him, who believed in his name, he gave power to become children of God" (Jn 1:12 RSV).

Faith is a dynamic with many levels of meaning on which we may reflect. We may best begin by thinking of faith as St. Maximus the Confessor saw it: "Faith is true knowledge, the principles of which are beyond rational demonstration; for faith makes real for us things beyond intellect and reason" (*First Century on Theology*, 9). For many moderns this explanation is a contradiction in terms. Those who accept only the intellect as the locus for ascertaining truth would say that there can be no knowledge beyond intellect and reason. For them rational argument, logical structures,

1

scientific experimentation or observation are the tools of knowledge; faith would be dismissed as 'subjective'. The great advances in science and technology by this methodology obscure for them the lack of ultimate answers to questions of origin or purpose or even the sheer wonderment of existence.

The Tradition of the Scriptures and the Fathers, however, affirms a more profound form of knowledge arising from deep within our being: a knowledge which remains outside the experience of those who value only the scientific method. It is this knowledge, born of the image of God found in everyone and the union with God of those who have put on Christ, which both generates the fullness of life in us and is the essense of that life as well. "Eternal life is this: to know you, the only true God, and Jesus Christ whom you have sent" (Jn 17:3 *JB*).

WE GROW IN FAITH

The Scriptural word for the way the believer puts one faith in God is *eis* ("into"). Our Lord told the apostles to "baptize [all nations] *into* the name of the Father and of the Son and of the Holy Spirit" (Mt 28:19). Accordingly at every baptism we sing, "All of you who have been baptized *into* Christ have put on Christ, alleluia" (cf Gal 3:27). Baptism "into" means most accurately that we belong to Him in whose name we have been baptized.[1] We more than belong; we "become" Christ as if we were embraced by Him. We express a faith that is more than just a belief in a set of propositions. It is a process of becoming what we believe, of moving towards union with the Trinity to whom we belong by baptism.

How far is this vision of faith from that of our own age! For many today faith is simple opinion about the appearance of truth: a matter of intellectual or emotional conviction. In the traditional Christian understanding, faith is nothing less than an event of ultimate reality, surpassing the limitations of the life of this world.

Yet there is an intellectual side to faith, a dimension of reasonableness or openness to logical expression. We can express our perception of what faith reveals through word-symbols, though these words remain inadequate to express the fulness of this reality. Thus the Church proclaims the mystery of God in specific terms in its profession of belief, the Nicene Creed, while reminding us that this is but a *Symbol* of the One we encounter through faith.

One aspect of the call to faith, then, is an invitation to make our own the Church's understanding of what God has shown us of Himself and what He has done to unite ourselves with Him. We are called not simply to a generic belief in God or religion, but to the faith of the Church. The first part of this presentation, "The Mystery Believed," sketches this mystery of the God who loves us and reveals Himself to us.

FAITH AS COMMUNAL

The Church has explicitly recognized the freedom involved in our acceptance of the gift of faith. A person can accept the fulness of faith only within the context of the community, but one must accept it freely. The modern age, on the other hand, has accepted a purely individualistic understanding of faith. "Real" faith is seen as a personal quest for the meaning of existence which is conducted in isolation, the journey of a lonely creature seeking union with God. The faith thus arrived at is viewed as completely subjective: a private matter whose truth is not important to anyone else.

This notion of rugged individualism, individual faith or private Christianity would simply be unknown in a traditional

3

mentality. The religion of the Scriptures and the Fathers is a corporate rather than an individual experience. God deals with individuals, to be sure, but He deals with them as part of a community, for faith is rather a gift of God first to the community of the Church and through the community to each individual person within it. Even those believers — prophets, hermits, monastics, not to mention Christ Himself — whose most exclusive and personal vocation called them forth from the life of the community were regularly sent back to the community with the fruit of their solitary experience.

Coming to such a living faith may involve a personal search, but even that quest arises from the operation of God in the depths of our being under the guidance of His Spirit. God has instilled in us a thirst for understanding, to seek the reasons of all things and ultimately to discover Him, the Creator. He is present on this path, even from its beginning, as a Reality deep within us. And whenever an aware and free human person is open in faith, then God is discovered as having been working within one from the beginning.

We also travel with others at our side to lead and teach, for the journey of faith takes place within a community whose culture gives form, expression, and witness to the presence of God as a living reality within it. And so, in Christian experience, a searcher for truth autonomous from others might exist theoretically until the search has led to Christ as the truth. At that point the believer can be described as having a deeply personal, but no longer private, faith. Individualistic Christianity is a self-contradiction.

Faith requires a commitment to Christ and also to His Church, since the Lord identified Himself with His people, the Church. "[God] has put all things under Christ's feet and has made Him, thus exalted, head of the Church which is His body, the fullness of Him who fills the universe in all its parts" (Eph 1:22–23 *NAB*). In "The Mystery Celebrated" that faith is shown to be no longer private. Its usual path to union with God is through baptism into His Church (cf. Mt 28:19–20; Mk 16:16). Thus faith leading to baptism, expressed in a positive way, forms "a chosen race, a royal priesthood, a holy nation, a people claimed for God's own" (1 Pt 2:9).

The Church realizes this communal understanding of Christianity most particularly in the liturgical synaxis. Divine worship is not simply a pious support to individual devotion; it is the arena in which we experience the Kingdom. When believers gather, God acts again in our midst making us the "community of the Holy Spirit." Here we experience through the remembrance and re-presentation of worship the saving acts of God-among-us. The second part of this handbook presents an overview of the liturgical tradition by which our Churches encounter the indwelling Spirit of God.

CONSEQUENCES OF FAITH

When God gives Himself to believers, He works a transformation in us. His gift mystically changes us and makes us into a new people through the power of the Spirit. This Spirit dwelling in us should affect our conscious lives as well to include the way we relate to others. The icon of the first Church drawn in the *Acts of the Apostles* shows us a people transfigured so that they "were looked up to by everyone" (Acts 2:47 *JB*). The *Letter to Diognetus* written at the end of the second century described this transformation as seen by a non-Christian: "They spend their lives on earth, but their citizenship is in heaven" (5:9). Thus true faith, which is the knowledge of God, never remains a detached intellectual exercise; it changes and transforms every aspect of our existence.

While the liturgical synaxis is the primary way in which the Church expresses and renews its communal faith, the daily life of

THE ALL-HOLY TRINITY

*God invites us into a relationship with Himself, but He reveals
Himself as a community of Father, Son and Holy Spirit. We are
invited into this primary community. The famous icon of the Holy
Trinity under the form of the hospitality of Abraham (cf Gn 18:1–
15) portrays three angels seated around a table. By the harmony
and blending of the lines of their bodies they form a circle, a unity
around the bread which suggests the Eucharist. The circle remains
open, inviting us to join this community of life and love. By our
hospitality to one another we become god-like. The psalmist
exclaimed, "Behold how good and how pleasant iit is, when
brethren dwell as one!" (Ps 132/133:1). The distinguishing mark
of the Christian faith remains love for one another (cf Jn 15:17; 1
Jn 4:7–13) in the image of the Trinity.*

the believer is the principal arena in which personal faith is exercised. The normal course of maturing faith leads to this call going outward into the community which receives the Gospel. Faith in Christ should make a difference not only for the individual believer but also for society as a whole.

In all ages Christian have given up their lives for the sake of faith or have devoted themselves in service to people. Their faith does make a difference. At the same time, the human weakness of Christians may have led them to act unworthily and thus be responsible for injustices against others.

"The Mystery Lived," our presentation's third section, attempts to show that the world is not outside our realm as Christians. Rather our mission is to the whole world, to call it to be transformed by Christ as all of life is now meant to be through the power of the Holy Spirit. Our knowledge of the physical universe leads to its transformation by technology. Likewise faith, based on knowledge and love of God, fulfills itself in the complete transformation of Christians. Through them the world created and loved by God is transformed by the action of the Holy Spirit into a new creation.

To know God as He has revealed Himself, to live in Him through the worshiping community, to serve Him in the working-out of our lives: this is our faith. Though our words remain inadequate to express the fullness of the reality to which we have been called, they do convey our openness to the mystery of God, even though that mystery has meaning beyond our apprehension of it.

For many, the life of faith may be a part of existence added to or superimposed on "real" life. For the Christian, knowing God is so intrinsic to living a human life and living in God is so integral to our very being that without Him we are not fully alive. We become complete persons through our relationship with God and others as we experience it in the faith community. In Christ we realize the true purpose of our nature as our humanity is completed and fulfilled. Henceforth, being human means being destined for divinity, led by the power of the Holy Spirit to be completely transformed after the model of "Him who fills all in all" (Eph 1:23).

1 — The Mystery of God

God is a mystery — until we admit this we cannot truly know Him. Any claim to have described Him or grasped Him has distorted Him. Today we who search out the secrets of the universe distrust unexplainable mysteries. We boldly seek to define God Himself, but He remains always beyond our power of understanding. Our concepts of God prove inadequate and clinging to them may even destroy our faith, as God exists beyond all the limitations of space and time which bind us. While we seek futilely to grasp at God, it is God who has sought us and revealed Himself in ways that we can only partly understand. And so what we do know of God comes from His revelations to humanity throughout our history.

From the beauty and order of nature, thinkers have argued to the existence of a creating principle. But faith requires a leap beyond this to knowledge of a loving and holy Creator. In truth, this can be done only by the favor and power of this Supreme Being. As material creatures, our direct experience of God is limited. As the Gospel says, "No one has ever seen God..." (Jn 1:18). God, however, has revealed Himself in many and varied ways. The Old Testament, as well as other religious traditions, describe many experiences of God. God speaks to the hearts of those who have faith and calls them to knowledge of Himself and of His loving plan for humanity. The testimony of various religions agrees on several attributes of God, our name for the Supreme Being. He is holy, meaning that He is completely other than us. He is infinite and transcendent. He is also good and loving to such a degree that we often call what is good "god-like."

As our experience of God grows through faith, we learn how all our ordinary concepts of God are so inadequate. If we think of Him merely as a logical necessity to explain the existence of the universe, then we fail to see the love at work in His plan. If we see

9

Him as an impersonal "force" in the universe, we cannot comprehend the words of the Psalmist, "Taste and see how good the Lord is" (Ps 33/34:9). If we see Him as someone to be invoked only when we are in trouble, then prayers of praise are meaningless. Very often it is such an inadequate concept of God which can hinder true knowledge of Him and even cause people to lose faith. When I deduce that God is not as I thought Him to be, I may conclude by denying there is a God of any kind.

JUST WHAT IS "MYSTERY"?

Mysteries both fascinate and frighten us — an instinctive fear of the unknown. Mysteries in the trivial sense of murder mysteries or of puzzles to be solved illustrate how we react to the unknown with a mixture of intrigue and alarm. Puzzles entice us with frustration or exhilaration, depending on our ability to solve them. Mysteries entertain with suspense and fear, forcing us to face our own frailty in the dangers of life and the unknowns of death. These trivial mysteries shed light on the profoundness of life itself as a mystery — both known and unknown, alluring and fearful.

Mystery for some is but a metaphor for what is not yet known, for superstition or ignorance. They believe the human mind will some day penetrate the secrets of the universe. However there are limits to our knowledge. How does one, as a part of creation, explain its very existence? — a task which requires an outside perspective. Science in this century has begun to recognize some of the theoretical boundaries of knowledge — of simultaneous position, and velocity of particles, of time as a variable limited by perspective. In the Book of Job we find something similar. God explains that some questions cannot be completely answered by man, "Who is this that confines words in his heart and thinks to conceal them from me? ... Where were you when I founded the earth? Tell me, if you have understanding" (Jb 38:2,4 LXX). We cannot answer why we are here, for we did not bring ourselves into existence; nor can we escape the mystery of death to which we are all called. Unless we believe that what we cannot know is meaningless, then we must face mystery.

The unknown is frightening but mystery is not simply the unknowable. It is also the hope that what is veiled can be uncovered, at least within the limitations of our nature. St. Paul was able to write, "God gave me the commission to preach among you His word in its fullness: that mystery hidden from ages and generations past, but now revealed to His holy ones" (Col 1:25–26). Mystery actually implies that answers to our ultimate questions do exist, although we cannot comprehend them. By the very fact of their existence, mysteries call us to transcend our human nature and point towards the infinite.

HIDDEN YET REVEALED

We should not despair of knowing anything about God, because He does reveal some of the mystery to us. This itself is an aspect of the mystery: how and why the Unknowable chooses to communicate Himself to us. "[God] causes the changes of the times and seasons, makes kings and unmakes them. He gives wisdom to the wise and knowledge to those who understand. He reveals deep and hidden things and knows what is in the darkness, for the light dwells with Him ... there is a God in heaven who reveals mysteries" (Dn 2:21–23, 28 NAB).

However much He reveals Himself, God remains mystery. In the Old Testament God tells Moses, "No one sees my face and still lives" (Ex 33:20). When Moses persisted and asked God for His name, the response was very mysterious. "God replied, 'I am who am'. This is what you shall tell the children of Israel: 'I AM sent me to You'" (Ex 3:14). God's revelation in this way expresses that what He is in Himself is not knowable through human limitation. The Source of all being or existence cannot be contained by a name. It serves as a caution for any of our concepts of God.

None of them can be perfect since we cannot comprehend God as He is in Himself.

The Tradition continued to stress the impossibility of any creature knowing God in the intimacy of His very being. St. Gregory of Nyssa believed that some knowledge of God is beyond human abilities:

> In speaking of God, when there is a question of His essence, then it is time to keep silence ... if the creature does not know itself, how can it explain things that are beyond it? Of such things it is the time to keep silence. Here silence is surely better."[1]

Other Fathers used negative language to describe the indescribable. St. John Chrysostom declared,

> Let us invoke Him as the inexpressible God, incomprehensible, invisible and unknowable; let us avow that He surpasses all power of human speech, that he eludes the grasp of every mortal intelligence, that the angels cannot penetrate Him, nor the seraphim see Him in full clarity, nor the cherubim fully understand Him, for He is invisible to the principalities and powers, the virtues and all creatures without exception; only the Son and the Holy Spirit know Him.[2]

St. Maximus the Confessor spoke of this transcendence of God in the strongest terms:

> God is one without beginning, incomprehensible, posessing completely the total potentiality of being, altogether excluding notions of when and how, inaccessible to all, and not to be known through natural image by any creature.[3]

In the anaphora of the Divine Liturgy of St. John Chrysostom we still pray the same thought: "You are God: ineffable, inconceivable, invisible, incomprehensible, ever existing yet ever the same." Theologians express this by saying that true knowledge of God is "apophatic": that the essence of God is beyond the understanding of any creature. We know God best when we come to Him by rejecting all false concepts of Him and by continually purifying our idea of God, even though what He is in Himself remains unknowable.

This awareness that we cannot completely grasp God is the very means which opens us to infinity. By realizing our imperfection, we can face always towards growth in virtue and wisdom. Perhaps the fact of our limitations is itself the key to our perfection. St. Gregory of Nyssa observed, "It may be that human perfection consists precisely in this constant growth in the good."[4]

IMAGE OF THE "BRIGHT CLOUD"

The surprising ways God has appeared illustrate the fullness of His nature. The glory of God often appears as a cloud signifying both clarity and darkness. When God made His covenant with Abraham, "a trance fell upon Abram and a deep, terrifying darkness enveloped him" (Gn 15:12 NAB). When God gave the law to Moses, "the glory of the Lord settled on Mount Sinai and the cloud covered it for six days. On the seventh day He called to Moses from the midst of the cloud" (Ex 24:16). The Lord appeared to the people of Israel as a cloud leading them from Pharaoh and through the desert to the Promised Land. The prophet Ezechiel described the presence of the Lord in the temple, "... the cloud filled the inner court, and the glory of the Lord rose from over the cherubim to the threshhold of the temple; the temple was filled with the cloud, and all the cloud was bright with the glory of the Lord" (Ez 10:4 NAB). When the Lord Jesus was transfigured in glory on Mount Tabor, He and the disciples were overshadowed by a bright cloud (cf. Mt 17:5).

The cloud is an image of our experience of God. Like a cloud, our knowledge of God is both bright and obscure. St. Gregory of Nyssa describes the process of how we are led through mystery to a greater awareness of God: "Next comes a closer awareness of hidden things, and by this the soul is guided through sense phenomena to the world of the invisible. And this awareness is a kind of cloud, which overshadows all appearances, and slowly guides and accustoms the soul to look towards what is hidden."[5]

The image of a cloud has been used widely to represent the mystery of our relationship with God, but God has revealed Himself to people in other ways too. God spoke to Moses "face to face, as a man speaks to his friend" (Ex 33:11). This simple statement shows how mystery does not hide, but reveals. We encounter God in the most ordinary human experiences. Many "theophanies" (manifestations of God) are in Scripture: some with fire, earthquake, and storms. Of course these are only simple images, since He is not one of those things. One of the most powerful theophanies in the Old Testament is the gentle appearance of God to Elijah on Mount Horeb. Elijah is told that God will pass by. A strong and heavy wind, an earthquake and a fire sweep through; but God was in none of these. "... after the fire [there was] a still small voice. And when Elijah heard it, he wrapped his face in his mantle and went out and stood at the entrance of the cave" (3/1 Kgs 19:12–13 RSV). The Lord spoke to him there. The still, small voice is our God speaking to our innermost being in quiet and gentleness.

These accounts of mankind's relationship to God remain profoundly true today. Claims of God's death or irrelevance are made by those who see no great divine manifestations in our modern social storms. Those looking for Him in the spectacular will miss His coming to us on His terms in mystery. Misunderstood images will betray us, for the true mystery of God is beyond all human comprehension.

ICON OF THE INVISIBLE

As Christians we believe that the fullness of the revelation of God is in our Lord Jesus Christ, whom we confess as "begotten of the Father before all ages, light of light, true God of true God, begotten not made, of one essence with the Father, through whom all things were made." Thus Jesus Himself is the only adequate

15

image of God. Whoever has seen Him has seen the Father (cf. Jn 14:9), for "He is the image of the invisible God" (Col 1:15).

The Tradition has identified Christ with the One who revealed His name to Moses. The mysterious name "Who-Am," *YHWH* in Hebrew, was translated as Ο ΩΝ (*o oon*) in the Greek Bible, the Septuagint. The fourth Gospel uses this same word for Christ: "No one has ever seen God. The only One [Ο ΩΝ], who is the same as God and is at the Father's side, he has made him known" (Jn 1:18, TEV). And so we write this Name in the halo surrounding Christ's head in icons and proclaim in our services, "Blessed is He-Who-Is [Ο ΩΝ], Christ our God..."

This revelation in Christ does not make God transparent to us. As Christians we accept the Lord Jesus Christ as the fullness of the revelation of God. Yet on the feast of the Transfiguration (August 6), the Church sings that, on Mount Tabor, Jesus revealed to His disciples only "as much of His glory as they could behold" (troparion). Further, His disciples "beheld as much of His glory as they could" (kontakion). God's self-revelation to us is limited, not by His love, but by our inability to grasp Him.

We can never know God completely, but we can always know Him increasingly better. As He draws us to Himself, we lose our childish and faith distorting concepts of God. We grow to know Him as loving and compassionate, giving Himself to us through Jesus Christ, revealed in the "mystery of mysteries,"[6] the Divine Liturgy. Here the Church enters into the saving life, death and resurrection of Jesus Christ. We glimpse the depth and breadth of the reality of God's love for us and His mystical union with us. While not replacing the broader relationship between God and humanity, the Liturgy becomes the transforming reality of that relationship. One may intellectually search for God, but He has already found us and united Himself to us in ways beyond our human understanding. We can hear the still, small voice of God speaking to our inner being across the ages with His timeless voice of love, and long to be "worthy to partake with a pure conscience

16

of [His] heavenly mysteries,"[7] and thus know Him in a way which surpasses the limitations of our mind.

We may end this consideration of the meaning of mystery with a prayer that concludes the Divine Liturgy of St. Basil and expresses our desire to enter ever more deeply into the mystery of God:

> O Christ our God, the mystery of Your plan has been completed and perfected, as far as in us lay. We have commemorated Your death; we have seen the figure of Your resurrection; we have been filled with Your endless life; we have enjoyed Your delights which cannot be exausted; and of which we beg You to deem us worthy in the age to come through the grace of the Father who has no beginning and of Your all-holy, good and life-giving Spirit...[8]

2 – The Mystery Revealed

"The Lord is God and has revealed Himself to us; blessed is He who comes in the name of the Lord." This refrain, so often sung in Matins, proclaims the abolition of the gulf separating God and His creation. This revelation, begun in the dim pre-history of the Jewish people, finds its completion in Christ, who is Himself the unity between heaven and earth, the divine and the human. By His incarnation, God has "lowered the heavens" and joined Himself to the human race. As the Church's Christmas services proclaim, "angels and people dance and rejoice together" for "the walls of partition have been broken down". All division has been overcome in the person of Christ, who is true God and true man. He has assumed all that is human, except for sin, and deified it in His person. Risen from the dead He has carried our human nature up to heaven where it is now seated at the right hand of the Father.

THE BIBLE: OUR RECORD OF GOD'S REVELATION

The mystery of God's plan in revealing Himself to His people is expressed concretely in the Sacred Scriptures, which record numerous milestones in the history of salvation. If our Christian faith is to be rooted deeply in the Gospel message and if we are to fully understand how Christ has fulfilled God's plan by restoring humanity to His likeness, we must turn back to the Old Testament. There we can follow the process of salvation from its announcement and on through the centuries. Then it was made ready in the lives of those people specially chosen by God, until at last it was fulfilled in Jesus Christ.

The Sacred Scriptures, or the Bible, is a series of "books" written by many different authors recording various stages in Jewish history. Inspired by God, its contents have reached us through human channels — coming first through the oral tradition of the people and then as written down by men seeking to convey God's truth through the literary means available to them. These biblical authors were completely human instruments used by God to record His activity. They were influenced by the age in which they lived and the circumstances of life around them. In bringing about these inspired writings, the Holy Spirit worked through their humanity and not in place of it. The reader must learn to discern the spiritual message being given without confusing it with the human elements in the work, which will become more recognizable through prayer and a proper study of the literary and historical background of the writer.

As we begin to read the Old Testament, we will notice the many different literary genres or methods used by the biblical authors: historical narration, law, oracle, poetry, didactic story, apocalyptic literature and others. Each literary form has a special significance and was chosen by the writer to express certain aspects of the divine reality that had been revealed to him. If we are to draw an adequate understanding of the inspired message from the passages we are reading, it is important to first determine which literary form the author has chosen to use. This attentiveness to literary form is critical for a proper understanding of the Sacred Scriptures.

REVEALED IN CREATION

The Old Testament, as arranged today, begins with the story of creation, even though Genesis (the Book of Beginnings) is not the oldest written book of the Bible. These narratives, along with the entire first eleven chapters of Genesis, form a special unit in the Bible — an inspired perspective on the "pre-history" of humanity up to the arrival of Abraham as a historical figure. This section uses elements from certain popular tales about the origins of humanity prevalent in the Middle East. Under the inspiration of the Holy Spirit, the authors retell these stories to reveal the religious truths of the fall and eventual salvation of the human race. Prominent

19

stories from this section include Adam and Eve, Cain and Abel, Noah and the Flood, and the Tower of Babel. In all these stories, we see how God reaffirms His love for mankind despite the disobedience in humanity.

The well-known creation stories (Gn 1:1–3:24) engage our imagination and raise fundamental human questions. This popularity has stimulated many additional stories, plays and commentaries, which sometimes even replace the Scriptural elements in popular imagination and art. The most obvious example is the forbidden fruit, usually depicted as an apple, although Genesis 2:17 calls it simply the fruit of the tree of the knowledge of good and evil.

In Genesis, creation is divided into six days. Current science asserts that the age of the universe is many *billions* of years, leading some people to dismiss the Genesis account as childish and inaccurate or to dismiss the whole Bible. Even today many controversies rage about the "truth" of Genesis — some dismissing it as myth and others defending an exaggeratedly literal interpretation. Unfortunately, both positions miss the real meaning of the Genesis creation as revealed by the Holy Spirit through the Fathers and councils of the Church.

A careful reading of the creation account reveals two separate stories. Chapters 1:1 to 2:4 describe the creation of the universe in six days with God resting on the seventh, the Sabbath. In this account, humanity is the last element of creation brought into being. The second version begins with the creation of humankind, represented by Adam and Eve, and their fall into sin (2:5 to 3:24). Scripture scholars today attribute these two stories to different Hebrew cultural traditions. The first is the "priestly" tradition; the second is the "Yahwist" tradition, so named because references to God use the name "YHWH" ("He-who-is") revealed to Moses.

Neither of these authors intended to write a history or science textbook in the modern sense, but rather to impart deeper religious truths about the origin of humanity and the world. The writing of a history would imply the presence of a human witness when God alone existed. The Hebrew authors were fully aware of the immensity of the chasm separating God and man and would not want to attempt definitive explanations of particular mechanisms God might choose.

The first narrative resembles, but corrects, other creation myths current in various world cultures in the centuries before Christ's birth. Many of these pagan sagas described creation as a struggle between the principle of goodness and light and the principle of darkness and chaos. When order and goodness triumphed, the beautiful world in which we live was organized. Such tales may have some kind of intermediary being as the one who brings forth order from a pre-existent chaos. Genesis, however, differs from the creation myths of the time in several key ways. Principally, God does not struggle as an equal with an evil and dark power. Rather, He creates by His word alone, and all that He made was good. This refrain is repeated after each phase until He creates man and woman and finds them *very* good.

Each item identified in the Genesis account was worshipped by some of the surrounding peoples — the sun, the moon, certain animals. The Scripture is saying that God made all these things and they are not gods. It is also saying that having false gods means that man ends up being like them and falling short of the true good that he could attain to. A basic and profound truth is taught here. All that exists has its ultimate origin in God, and comes forth from His creative power as truly good. Even so, its created splendor is but a pale reflection of the ineffable beauty of The One Who Is, the source of all that is. Only one God exists and He has no equal.

The second creation story presents the truth of how humanity lost its friendship with God. Adam and Eve become the prototypes of the whole human race. God's creative intention for the human race was for people to be on intimate terms of friendship with Him and each other. "It is not good for the man to be alone"

(2:18 NAB). The account depicts the created state as a life of perfection with neither guilt nor death. Yet, humanity did not remain faithful to God's plan. They ate of the forbidden tree of the knowledge of good and evil and lost innocence and incorruptibility. God then banished them from the tree of life and from the garden.

This narrative wrestles with the fundamental faith issue: how did humanity become weak, prone to evil and unable to refrain from sin and malice? Its roots lie in our basic pattern of disobedience to God from the very beginning. We try to decide what is good or evil on our own terms, thereby usurping God's prerogative. Death, evil and misery follow.

This latter creation story forms the foundation for understanding God's salvation through Jesus Christ in the New Testament. In Rom 5:12–21, Jesus is called the new Adam who has replaced the old Adam's pattern of disobedience by faithfulness to the Father. He thereby gives us new access to the tree of life — identified by the Church as the wood of the cross — which leads to the glorious resurrection.

Similarly, the first chapter of the Gospel of St. John presents the mystery of Christ as a new creation. St. John identifies Jesus as the Word of God (*Logos*) active in creation ("through Him all things came into being, and apart from Him nothing created came to be" — Jn 1:3 NAB). This Logos is described as entering the world in the incarnation to restore us to friendship with the Father. "Of His fullness we have all received — grace following upon grace. For while the law was given through Moses, grace and truth came through Jesus Christ" (Jn 1:16–17). This Gospel, read in the Byzantine Divine Liturgy on the feast of Pascha (Easter), proclaims our restoration to life in the risen Christ and the beginning of a new Creation. Pascha is the "First day of the week, the Feast of Feasts," celebrating our return to paradise, where we are now invited to partake of the Body and Blood of Christ, fruit of the Cross, the tree of life, "for the forgiveness of sins and life everlasting."

Jesus' divine nature, the creative force of the Trinity, is described as the Word or *Logos*. St. John profoundly relates, "Apart from him nothing created came to be ... whatever came to be in him, found life" (1:3–4). This recalls Genesis 1 where God spoke as He brought into being the diverse components of life. This Word is eternal, "present to God in the beginning" (Jn 1:2). Having beheld the goodness of the original plan and the pain of sin's interference with this plan, the Word unites with humanity to save creation and to direct us back to our true home. Sin (the darkness) is unable to understand this mystery nor to conquer it (Jn 1:5). No created thing existing in time (itself created) is able to defeat the Lord who was in the beginning and became flesh. By God's new and radical gift of Himself to us, we may now freely choose to return to our original destiny, which is with the Trinity. The Holy Spirit of God hovered over the waters at creation giving life. This movement and brooding of the Spirit has not ceased to bring new fullness of life at each successive step of the creation process. Thus the Spirit is still at work, unfolding God's truth in the Church.

These stories of creation are true in the most profound sense. They give us an understanding of the condition of humanity and its relationship to God, our Creator. They do not purport to explain the scientific existence of the physical universe. Serious attempts are made at times to square the Genesis accounts with the observation and theories of contemporary science concerning material creation. But conformity to science is irrelevant to the religious truth of Genesis. Science is attempting to answer questions different from those of faith. Correspondingly, the story of Adam and Eve need not be verifiable by modern methods of determining historical truth. Its message, however, is clear. Failing to respect the Genesis author's intention and insisting inappropriately on its literal meaning may actually distort the truth of this message.

The Biblical creation accounts relate that all which God has made is very good. This goodness can lead us to love of God. In complementary fashion faith in God sheds new light upon the meaning of creation. Without God, creation is at best meaningless or perhaps absurd. St. Paul described God to the philosophers of Athens:

> From one stock he made every nation of mankind to dwell on the face of the earth. It is he who set limits to their epochs and fixed the boundaries of their regions. They were to seek God, yes to grope for him ... though he is not really far from any one of us. 'In him we live and move and have our being' as some of your own poets have put it, 'for we too are his offspring'" (Acts 17:26–28 NAB).

The Biblical story of creation is an affirmation that our Creator is the intimate, caring God who is involved with everything happening, for "not a single sparrow falls to the ground without your Father's consent" (Mt 10:29 NAB). How much greater is His concern for us, who are made in His image and likeness and are able to marvel at Creation's beauty and to praise the one Creator. It is to us who can perceive and express the beauty of God's work that "The heavens declare the glory of God and the firmament proclaims his handiwork" (Ps 18/19:1).

HUMANITY IN GOD'S IMAGE AND LIKENESS

In its second story of creation, Genesis distinguishes between humanity and all of God's other works. We share the same origin and destiny of all created matter, but at the same time we are radically different. We exist in the "image and likeness" of God (Gn 1:26).

Countless Jewish and Christian thinkers have sought to explain what it might mean to be in God's image. Some have stressed the dominion and stewardship over creation God gives us (cf Gn 1:26). While clearly subordinate to Him, we share in His lordship as free beings with responsibilities and control. Others have accented our mental and spiritual qualities, particularly our free will as marking us in God's image.

Many Fathers of the Church used "image" and "likeness" to help describe our relationship with God. For them, "image" designated that indestructible similarity to God that is at the heart of our nature. These Fathers saw this image in many aspects of the human person, including our freedom, our rationality, our dominion over the world, and our immortality. Some Eastern Christians in particular have looked to our creation as a community ("male and female He created them") as reflecting the Trinitarian essence of God. Still others have seen the entire human person as like God: body, emotions and intellect.

For the Fathers, the word "likeness" designated our union with God, by the power of the Holy Spirit. They saw this harmony with God illustrated in Genesis by the description of Adam and Eve enjoying fellowship with God in the garden. In their view image and likeness are complementary. Made in God's image, we are free; and as free, we affirm our likeness in union with God. However, Adam sinned and chose not to be "like God." He lost the likeness in us and marred the image. The image of God in us remains always as the basis for restoring friendship with God and for destined union with Him.

Christ repaired the damage of Adam's sin, "For if many died through one man's trespass, much more have the grace of God and the free gift in the grace of that one man, Jesus Christ, abounded for many" (Rom 5:15 RSV). Christ, the perfect "image of the invisible God, the first-born of all creatures" (Col 1:15), restores the divine likeness to humanity when He became "like his brethren in every respect ... yet without sin" (Heb 2:17; 4:15 RSV).

In the new creation ushered in by Christ, the divine image in humanity is fulfilled. While Christ is the perfect image of God, the Christian is the image of Christ. Our nature in the image of God is affirmed and we are now able to recover the divine likeness. It is

25

now possible to return to the original harmony of life as it was before the fall. We can act from our true human nature after the image and likeness of God. We can choose to give ourselves back to God by the grace of the Spirit. Our journey of life can become, as St. Irenaeus said, a steady "progress towards a future full of promise." We can be truly human again because we can soar towards union with God.

ADAM WEEPING BEFORE PARADISE.

THE FALL OF MANKIND

Genesis continues with further stories concerning Adam and Eve, Cain and Abel, Noah and the Flood, and the Tower of Babel. These accounts all have certain elements in common. Each tells of humanity's fall from intimate friendship with God through disobedience. Adam and Eve eat of the fruit of the tree of the knowledge of good and evil in order to be like God. Cain kills Abel out of envy. His sacrifice is rejected by God and Abel's is accepted. The world is destroyed by a flood, because "the Lord saw how man's wickedness on earth was increasing, and how no desire that his heart conceived was ever anything but evil" (Gn 6:5-6). The tower of Babel is built out of the pride of the people. In their minds, they could accomplish anything they wanted without depending on their Creator; they could reach God on their own terms.

Humanity's choice not to participate in God's plan for the world results in disaster. Adam and Eve lose their companionship with God and their access to the tree of life. They are condemned to eventual death: the men to work by sweat and toil and the women to experience pain in childbearing. They feel the pangs of guilt and lose the beautiful homeland that had been under their dominion. By his act of murder, Cain becomes a person despised, a wanderer without a real home in this world. As sin spreads, God destroys nearly the whole race He had made and restarts it with Noah. Through pride human beings lose the ability to communicate and become strangers to one another "scattered all over the earth" (Gn 11:9). The results of sin are always death, alienation, and confusion. These tales succinctly tell the story of human history. From the very beginning we developed a habit of acting contrary to our true well-being by rejecting the plan of the Creator. In vain and false attempts to become like God on our own terms, we lost our true likeness to God.

Another theme in these primitive stories is the introduction of sin by an evil influence from outside human nature. The serpent tempts Adam and Eve through lies and deception, telling them that, if they ignore God's warning, they "will be like gods ..." (Gn 3:5). Rv 12:9 identifies the serpent with the devil, who is "a liar by nature — a liar and the father of lies" (Jn 8:44). Humanity was created good, destined for union with God and for the love and help of one another. Our impulse towards evil comes from the outside, from that personal evil spirit we call Satan. St. Paul observed, "Our battle is not against human forces but against the principalities and powers, the rulers of this world of darkness, the evil spirits in the regions above" (Eph 6:12 NAB).

The existence of the devil as the source of evil does not remove our own responsibility for our actions. Yet, we cannot do what is evil without some deception. We must believe it to be for our benefit, at least in the short run. When we decide to do wrong, we make this deception a form of "self-deception," the condition for all sin. We become followers of the "evil one" rather than of Christ, the Light of the world. We become ourselves "people of the lie."

This term, "people of the lie," was used as the title of a book by M. Scott Peck. In a powerful paragraph he lists lies that are told today. Some are quite common beliefs which show that these stories of humanity's beginnings contain vital truths about our life situation. He lists as the lies of Satan:

> Humans must defend themselves in order to survive and cannot rely on anything other than themselves in their defense; everything is explainable in terms of negative and positive energy (which balance out to zero), and there is no mystery in the world; love is a thought and has no objective reality; death is the absolute end to life — there is no more; all humans are motivated by money, and if this appears not to be the case, it is only because they are hypocrites; to compete for money, therefore, is the only intelligent way to live. [1]

The spread of evil derives from creation's loss of purpose or direction resulting from man's disobedience. Dominion over the created world was entrusted to man, who was made in God's own image and likeness. Man chose instead to be controlled by the world and forfeited his freedom. Maximus the Confessor interprets Adam and Eve's "garments of skin" (Gn 3:21) as a change in humanity's situation involving a greater dependence upon the animal side of existence. Mankind's purpose to lead creation to God was thwarted by succumbing to the desires of material sensation. The world became a prison of constant temptation, through which the "prince of this world" brings death as the inheritance of the Fall. Individual sin could be seen as a consequence of mortality, which makes man anxious about what he should eat or drink (cf. Mt 6:31). In baptism parents can transmit immortal life to their mortal child as a weapon to fight sin.

Besides explaining the existence of evil in this world, these first chapters of Genesis also pre-announce the coming of salvation. In the first story of creation, "God looked at everything he had made, and he found it very good" (1:31 NAB). Even after the fall, Eve becomes "the mother of all the living" (3:20). God curses the serpent making mankind its enemy: "I will put enmity between you and the woman, and between your offspring and hers; He will strike at your head, while you strike at his heel" (3:15 NAB). Even Cain is given protection by the Lord (4:10–11). After the flood destroys all the inhabitants of the earth, God makes a new covenant with Noah, telling his family, "Be fertile and multiply and fill the earth ... abound on earth and subdue it ... never again shall all bodily creatures be destroyed by the waters of a flood" (9:1,7,11). The ultimate promise is that God is a loving provider, who "did not turn away from His creation, nor forget the work of his hands." (Liturgy of St. Basil, ref. Ps 137/138:8)

ECHOES IN OUR WORSHIP

The themes of this first part of Genesis have become prominent in our celebration of God's salvation in the worship of the Church. In the eucharistic prayers (*anaphoras*) of the Divine Liturgies we proclaim that, after we had fallen, God has raised us up again in Jesus Christ. At Christmas we celebrate Christ as the "tree of life," recalling that from which Adam and Eve were banned (Gn 3:24): "... the Tree of life has blossomed forth from the Virgin in the cave. Her womb has become a spiritual Paradise wherin the divine Fruit was planted — and if we eat of it we shall live and not die like Adam. Christ is coming forth to bring back to life the likeness that had been lost in the beginning" (Troparion, Preparation for Christmas).

The reopening of Paradise is a frequent theme in the Church's prayer. In the kontakion for the Veneration of the Holy Cross during Lent we sing, "No longer does the flaming sword guard the gates of Eden, for the Cross of the Lord has put it out wonderously. The power of death has been broken, the victory of Hades wiped out and You, O my Savior, have stood up and called out to those in the Abyss [Hades]: 'Enter again into paradise.'" One hymn for the Exaltation of the Cross (September 14) proclaims, "Lifted high upon the cross, O Master, You raised up with Yourself Adam and our entire fallen nature... He who by a tree deceived our forefather Adam, is by the cross himself deceived ... Today the death that came to man through eating of the tree, is made of no effect through the cross ..." Another declares, "On [the Cross] Christ, the King of glory, freely stretched out His hands. By this He raised us up to our former happiness, which we had lost because of the ancient Enemy and the bitter pleasure [the eating from the tree] that exiled us from God." All these images echo the Gospel where the Lord opens Paradise to the good thief from His cross (Lk 23:42).

The Genesis stories also figure in the Byzantine theology of Baptism. By our faith in Christ Jesus and our acceptance of His call to baptism (ref. Mt 28:16-20), we really and truly become a part of a new creation as St. Gregory the Theologian explains:

> To be utterly sinless belongs to God ... but to sin is human ... therefore, the Master did not think it right to leave his creature unaided, or to neglect its danger of separation from himself, but just as he gave existence to that which did not exist, so he gave new creation to that which did exist, a diviner

creation and a loftier than the first ... such is the grace and power of baptism, not an overwhelming of the world as of old, but a purification of the sins of each individual, and a complete cleansing from all the bruises and stains of sin.[2]

St John Chrysostom compares the new creation of baptism to the original creation of Genesis: "Then [God] made man to the image of God; now He makes him one with God Himself ... He gave the first man Paradise for his dwelling; now He has opened heaven to us."[3] The nakedness of the candidate is contrasted with the nakedness of Adam and Eve: "There was nakedness then and there is nakedness now. But in the old covenant, after Adam sinned, he was naked because he had sinned; in the new, the candidate is stripped that he may be freed from sin."[4] The baptismal robe becomes our clothing in Christ (Gal 3:27), replacing the shame of Adam and Eve at their nakedness in the garden of Eden (Gn 3:27).

ABRAHAM AND THE ISRAELITES

Genesis continues with the story of Abraham, ancestor of the Israelites and father of all who believe. Abraham had a series of profound personal experiences of the God of mystery: "a trance fell upon him, and a deep terrifying darkness enveloped him" (Gn 15:12). Abraham was called to put all his trust in God. He and his wife Sarah were old and childless, yet he was told by God that he would become the father of a great nation. He, in turn, was to leave his home and his clan for a new and strange land. Abraham would no longer see God as the local patron of a particular region, but the God of all creation.

God took the initiative in entering into a relationship with Abraham and his descendants. In this God was making a covenant with all humanity. St. Paul would later explain this covenant from a Christian perspective:

Consider the case of Abraham; he "believed God, and it was credited to him as justice." This means that those who believe are sons of Abraham. Because Scripture saw in advance that God's way of justifying the Gentiles would be through faith, it foretold this good news to Abraham: "All nations shall be blessed in you." Thus it is that all who believe are blessed along with Abraham, the man of faith (Gal 3:6–9 NAB).

The story of Abraham is read at Vespers and at the Presanctified Liturgies of the fourth and fifth weeks of Great Lent. Especially stressed are his call to a new land, the covenant of circumcision (replaced in Christianity by baptism), and his willingness to sacrifice his son Isaac. God refused to accept this sacrifice, perhaps as a sign that human sacrifice was repugnant to Him. What is important is Abraham's complete openness to God, who would later give us His only Son who would be sacrificed for us on the cross.

Sometimes an icon of the sacrifice of Isaac is placed over the Table of Preparation to remind us of Abraham's faith. In this it invites us to show ourselves to be "descendants of Abraham" by giving ourselves to God; as we pray in the litanies: "let us commend ourselves and one another and our whole lives to Christ our God."

MOSES AND THE EXODUS

Central to the entire Old Testament is the supreme redemptive act of God, by which He lead the Israelites out from their slavery in Egypt. This event, called the *exodus*, begins with the enslavement of Abraham's descendants in Egypt by a pharaoh "who knew nothing of Joseph" (Ex 1:8). For political reasons, the people were reduced to slavery by a pattern of sinful behavior that sought power for the self and hated those who were different. This injustice was a manifestation of the evil that had entered the human race.

God looked with compassion on the people so caught and revealed Himself as a redeemer by calling the prophet Moses to lead them out of servitude "into a good and spacious land, a land flowing with milk and honey" (Ex 3:8). He identified Himself to Moses, "I am the God of your father ... the God of Abraham, the God of Isaac, the God of Jacob ... I have seen the affliction of my people in Egypt and have heard their cry of complaint against their slave drivers ..." (Ex 3:6–7).

MOSES

The exodus is the model for all of God's relationships to His people. In it we encounter a God who takes the initiative in loving us and calling us to His friendship. As the Lord passed before him, Moses was moved to cry out, "The Lord, the Lord, a merciful and gracious God, slow to anger and rich in kindness and fidelity, continuing in his kindness for a thousand generations, and forgiving wickedness and crime and sin" (Ex 34:6–7). In later years the prophets would never forget how God deals with the human race: He remains faithful even though His people sin.

33

The experience of the exodus was also the pledge of a covenant between God and His people Israel. He who brought them out of Egypt called them to worship Him alone. This great commandment given to them was to be repeated daily as a prayer, "Hear, O Israel! The Lord is our God, the Lord alone! Therefore, you shall love the Lord, your God, with all your heart, and with all your soul and with all your strength" (Dt 6:4–5).

The story of exodus is experienced by the Church in a new way during the Great and Holy Week in which we celebrate the Lord Jesus' death and resurrection. We proclaim our belief that "a new Passover has shone upon us" (Paschal Stichera). Christ fulfilled the spiritual meaning of the exodus by freeing the whole human race from slavery to sin. This salvation is far more universal than the exodus from a physical slavery in one distant place and time. To proclaim this new covenant, Jesus established the Eucharist to fulfill the Passover meal which the Jews solemnly ate to remember the events of the exodus.

Many details of the exodus account are models for the way God works in our lives. To find the promised land, the people of Israel had to wander through a desert for forty years. This came to indicate the time of preparation we need as we wait for God to act. Thus Moses fasted in the desert for forty days before receiving the ten commandments. Elijah fasted for forty days in the desert before He came into God's presence. Jesus fasted for forty days when he turned back the temptations of the devil. In the same way the desert or the mountain became privileged places for encountering God. These places separate us from distractions and bring us into the silence where we can hear the quiet voice of God. Jesus would reveal His divinity to Peter, James and John on a high mountain when He was transfigured before them. Moses and Elijah appeared present at this event as representatives of the Law and the Prophets becuase they had experienced God in similar ways.

To find the presence of God in our own lives, we too need some kind of "desert experience." The Church offers us such experiences in its fasting seasons, especially the forty day Great Fast before the feast of our Lord's resurrection (Lent).

The desert also contains an element of danger. The Israelites' desert experience was not all positive; in fact it resulted from a weakness of their faith. The barrenness of the desert is a image of the struggle with the evil one and his temptation. In the desert our Lord struggled with Satan, and many early Christians took up a life in the desert. They became the first monks and nuns, founding a new and holy way of life in which to struggle with evil and defeat it. Their goal was to become completely open to union with God. This struggle is called *asceticism*, the life of repentance.

Every person who wishes truly to follow after Christ must engage in some form of repentance. This way of life entails risks, but without repentance we cannot grow in wisdom and love. The parable of the talents warns of the dangers of false security (Mt 25:14–30; Lk 19:12–27).

The exodus was also the occasion for a fuller revelation of God as One who does not deal with us impersonally, but as persons. To Moses He reveals His glory (Ex 33:18–19) and spoke to him "face to face, as a man speaks to his friend" (Ex 33:11). The Lord even gives Moses His name, "I am Who Am," (in Hebrew, *Yahweh*). The Lord called Moses His "intimate friend." The whole story of exodus tells how God is deeply concerned about His people, the Hebrews, and, by extension, us. The giving of the Law centered upon the ten commandments as a part of God's intimate loving concern for persons, a guide to a way of life that would avoid evil and fulfill us personally. They are less a law than knowledge about the true path to God.

The account of the exodus makes no attempt to glorify the people of Israel, and deliberately underlines the faults and failings of its leaders and of the people themselves. Exodus puts God at the center of the story of Israel, the merciful Lord who hearkens to the helpless and brings them to salvation. A new horizon of light and

hope is opened up as the redeemer God encounters His people in
their enslavement and suffering. God becomes the chief protagonist
of this story, always ready to redeem and rescue. Rather than a
being a secular history of their origins, Exodus is a proclamation of
"good news" that provides the texture of the whole religious and
ethical-social life of the Jewish people. Their religious and moral
ideal would remain that of walking with God.

The number of Israelites who actually left Egypt were few,
but they became representative of all who would follow. Through
their Passover sharing of faith, later generations have had the
opportunity to participate in the grace conferred upon those few.
The same is true for us Christians as well. As many as we are, we,
too, participate in the grace of the Paschal Mystery, celebrated in
each Divine Liturgy and renewed in the liturgical services of Holy
Week and Easter. When we participation in these celebrations with
faith, we are identified with the "Passover" of Jesus Christ and
enjoy the saving effects of His death and resurrection.

GOD OF THE COVENANT

The story of the Old Testament tells of the relationship
entered into between God and His people. This relationship was
called a "covenant," or solemn agreement, rather like a formal
treaty. Of the various covenants in the Old Testament, the greatest
one is the covenant made with the Israelites through the prophet
Moses. On this occasion the people were liberated by God from
slavery in Egypt and were led to a promised land. In return they
were to worship the one, true God and they were given the Ten
Commandments and the Law, as recorded in the first five books of
the Bible.

Of the other covenants the one with Adam declared that
human beings would be given paradise and friendship with God if
they would not eat of the tree of the knowledge of good and evil.
The covenant with Noah declared that God would never again

destroy the world by a flood. The covenant with Abraham testified that God would make Abraham the father of a great nation, if in turn his male children and descendants would be circumcised.

In these covenants, God's promise is guaranteed by His own witness: "When God made his promise to Abraham, he swore by himself, having no one greater to swear by" (Heb 6:13). Despite all the sins and failures of humanity, God remains absolutely faithful to His promises, simply because they are His word. They may take centuries of our time before they are fulfilled, as with as God's promise to Abraham. They may yet to be fulfilled, as in the promise of the universal resurrection. But God's unfailing fidelity to His word remains a sign of hope to us, especially when we feel He is indifferent.

JUDGES AND KINGS

Once in the promised land, the people of Israel considered themselves to be under the immediate sovereignty of their God. They formed a loose confederacy of tribes led politically by various "judges", and led religiously by prophets and priests. The most well-known judge is Samson whose story is told in Judges 13–16. Despite the periodic emergence of a judge, the ultimate ruler of the chosen people could be only the Lord Himself. Eventually, however, the people felt themselves to be at a disadvantage with respect to the neighboring kingdoms. They demanded, "There must be a king over us. We too must be like other nations, with a king to rule us and to lead us in warfare and fight our battles" (1 Kgs/1 Sam 8:20 NAB).

As a result of these demands, the prophet Samuel chose Saul and anointed him as king (1 Kgs/1 Sam 10:1). Saul would eventually prove to be an unworthy king, and the reign would be given to David. He established the basic kingdom and even set up a fair sized empire over neighboring regions. David was a very complicated character, who did much wrong; still he was faithful to

God's trust until the end of his life. The Scriptures would be able to call him, "the anointed of the God of Jacob, the sweet psalmist of Israel" (2 Kgs/2 Sam 23:1 RSV). Later kings were often not faithful, but God remained faithful to the promises He had made to David and to His people.

The choosing of a king is portrayed in the Old Testament as a failure of confidence in the leadership of the invisible God, but the Lord transformed this new situation into the beginning of new blessings. Part of the mystery of God's love for us is that He continually brings good from what is bad. Final salvation for all the world came through the life and death of His only Son. The kingship of Israel was made the office of Messianic hope. It was promised to David through the prophet Nathan that "your house and your kingdom shall endure forever before me; your throne shall stand firm forever" (2 Kgs/2 Sm 7:16 NAB). This and similar passages became the basis for the hope of the people that one day a Messiah would come, sent by God, to lead them to salvation.

"MESSIAH WILL COME"

Messiah in Hebrew and *Christ* in Greek mean "the Anointed One." Thus, Jesus Christ is the equivalent of "Jesus the Messiah." Anointing with oil was a sign of God's election. At His baptism in the Jordan River, Jesus was revealed as the Messiah because He is God's chosen and favored one.

Priests, prophets, and kings would be anointed as a sign of God's favor and of the gift of the Holy Spirit. The future Messiah was expected to combine the three roles, which Jesus Christ did, although in a new and spiritual sense. The Epistle to the Hebrews describes Jesus as the eternal High Priest, who offered the sacrifice of His own blood, and "is seated at the right hand of the throne of the Majesty in heaven" (8:1). The Gospels often describe Jesus as greater than John the Baptist, who was clearly a prophet in the classic mold. In this light, the meaning of the people's questions to

Jesus inquiring whether He was "one of the prophets" can be understood. Finally, Jesus proclaims the kingdom of God, though it was not to be a reign of worldly glory or power (Jn 18:36). Thus the importance placed in the Gospel of St. Matthew that Jesus is the "Son of David" becomes clear. He is truly the heir and fulfillment of all God's promises.

THE PROPHETS: CONSCIENCE OF ISRAEL

The role of the prophets in the Old Testament deserves special attention. A large portion of the Old Testament is the record of the sayings of the prophets. More than any other group, they were responsible for forming the people's awareness of God's plan for the human race and of how one should act to fulfill it. The prophets were chosen by God to speak in His name and given special gifts and authority to fulfill this mission. This is why the prophets' teachings often begin with the words, "Thus says the Lord..."

The common conception of a prophet emphasizes foretelling the future. This aspect of the prophets' ministry flowed from their primary ones of preaching and exhortation. If their pronouncement of God's plan was true, the consequences of not heeding it must follow. Their predictions of the future were a seal of authenticity to their message.

The prophets were the people's "conscience." They continually preached of God's faithfulness to His covenants and exhorted the people to be faithful. Often the prophets' moral teachings would upset the authorities who were less interested in the Law of God than in their own positions. When King Ahab met the prophet Elijah, his first words were, "Is it you, you disturber of Israel?" (3/1 Kgs 18:16). The prophets' persistence in this role often led to persecution and death, down to the time of John the Baptist who was beheaded for decrying the immorality of King

Herod. The Lord Jesus Himself was crucified in part for challenging the behavior of the religious leaders.

Jesus condemned the people for not listening to the prophets: "This generation will have to account for the blood of all the prophets shed since the foundation of the world" (Lk 11:50 NAB). In this same way we are reproached for not heeding the voice of Jesus. At the Great Hours on Good Friday, the Byzantine Churches put these words into the mouth of Jesus on the Cross, "O my people, what have I done to you? How have I wearied you? ... What have I done to you, and how have you repaid me?"

Scriptural evidence indicates that the role of prophet continued into apostolic times. A prophet named Agabus foretells Paul's arrest and trial by the Romans (Acts 21:10–11). In the Christian prophetic book of Revelation an angel tells John, "I am merely a fellow servant with you and your brothers the prophets" (22:9). *The Didache*, written in the first century, also describes the role of the prophet in the Christian community as one who "speaks forth in the spirit" (11:7).

It was never easy to tell true prophets from false prophets who misled. The Epistles of St. John and the Didache contain rules for distinguishing false from true prophets, based on their way of life and the integrity of their teaching. The prophetic role became subsumed into the episcopacy quite early. This development seems to have been underway by the time of the Didache (15:1). The present prayer for the ordination of a bishop recalls his prophetic role: "As You strengthened Your holy apostles and prophets, do you, the same Master of all ... strengthen him whom You have chosen ... to the episcopate."

Prophets are needed for all times. They stirred up the awareness of Israel to realize that God's actions were not limited to earlier times but applied to the present and the future as well. The prophets foretold the coming of the Messiah and how He could be recognized. When Jesus came, the people constantly checked back to the prophecies to verify His authenticity. St. Matthew and the other Gospels show Christ fulfilling all the Messianic prophecies. One of the most important passages spoke of the suffering Messiah and foretold many details of the crucifixion (Is 52:13 — 53:12). Such suffering was not part of the popular understanding of the Messiah. The fulfillment of this prophecy added additional power to the authenticity of Jesus as the Christ, once this preconception was confronted.

The duty of prophets today is to proclaim that God is still acting and that He will come again in the future. The Holy Spirit is "God-with-us" today, the Paraclete promised by Christ to be with us always (cf. Jn 14:16). In the Creed we profess that it is the Spirit who speaks through the prophets. He is the One through whom the prophetic office is exercised and who calls us constantly to renewal. St. Simeon the New Theologian pointed out:

> It is by the Holy Spirit that everyone experiences the resurrection, by which I do not mean the ultimate resurrection of the body ... I am speaking about the spiritual regeneration and resurrection of dead souls that takes place in a spiritual fashion every day *(Catechesis* 6:10).

JESUS, THE WORD INCARNATE

"In times past, God spoke in fragmentary and varied ways to our fathers through the prophets; in this, the final age, he has spoken to us through his Son" (Heb 1:1 NAB). This opening statement of the Epistle to the Hebrews reflects the Church's understanding that the whole of the Scriptures illustrates God's continuing work for the salvation of humanity. In this work the highpoint is the person and mission of Jesus Christ, "the image of the invisible God, the first-born of all creatures" (Col 1:15), in whom the mystery of God hidden from the ages was revealed (cf Col 2:25–28).

The mission of Jesus was to restore humanity to its friendship with God: a relationship which had been lost by sin. "God, in Christ, was reconciling the world to himself, not counting men's transgressions against them" (2 Cor 5:19). He did more than remove the enmity between God and humanity. He became man like us, "he made himself poor though he was rich, so that you might become rich by his poverty" (2 Cor 8:9). We would "become sharers of the divine nature" (2 Pt 1:4). St. Athanasius comments on these passages by saying, "[Christ] was made man that we might be made God" (*On the Incarnation*, 54).

The concept of deification is central to God's plan of salvation, but it is accomplished only in conformity with His plan. The temptation of the devil in the Garden of Eden was, "The moment you eat of the fruit [of the tree of the knowledge of good and evil] your eyes will be opened and you will be like gods" (Gn 3:5 NAB). The devil lied, since being God-like is not in humanity's powers apart from God. Through the mystery of Christ, God undid the damage of sin and restored our destiny, now revealed to be deification. By becoming a man, Christ made human nature itself share in the Godhead. We cannot become God by nature, but "if anyone is in Christ, he is a new creation" (2 Cor 5:17). Hence, "they may both be and be called gods through the gift of grace, since God as a whole fills them entirely and does not let any part of them be empty of His presence."[5]

The mystery of deification goes hand in hand with the New Testament doctrine of the incarnation ("being-made-flesh"). The Church has always affirmed, at the very center of its faith, that in Jesus, God became man. In the fifth century, the Council of Chalcedon (the Fourth Ecumenical Council) declared, "our Lord Jesus Christ is to be confessed as one and the same person, perfect in Godhead and perfect in humanity, truly God and truly man, consisting of a rational soul and body, one in substance with the Father as regards His Godhead, and one in substance with us as regards His humanity; made in all things like unto us, sin only excepted." This confession restates what is found in the Gospels and the Pauline Epistles: "Though he was in the form of God, he did not deem equality with God something to be grasped at. Rather, he emptied himself and took the form of a slave, being born into the likeness of men" (Phil 2:6–7 NAB). This magnificent passage, in turn, was possibly a quotation by St. Paul of a liturgical hymn used by the apostolic Christians.

This understanding of Jesus as both God and man has been expressed in a variety of ways over the centuries. We profess that same faith when we say the Nicene Creed: "I believe ... in one Lord, Jesus Christ, ... who for us men and for our salvation, came down from heaven, and was incarnate from the Holy Spirit and the Virgin Mary, and became man." We hear this same theme expressed in the Divine Liturgy of St John Chrysostom which itself quotes Jn 3:16, "You [the Father] so loved Your world that You gave Your only-begotten Son, that everyone who believes in Him should not perish, but should have life everlasting." Nonetheless these statements stand in continuity with the apostles' experiences of the Lord as truly "the Son of God."

Seeing deification as the purpose of the incarnation has helped the Church keep a balance in expressing its faith. The Church has defined that Jesus was truly a man, like us in every way except sin. We do not believe that His divinity totally absorbed His humanity and rendered it insignificant. This would be equivalent to saying that we cannot be raised up and be saved by His incarnation. On the other hand, we cannot accentuate the humanity of Jesus so that the divinity becomes irrelevant. We would make Him simply a holy and wise teacher; but union with Him would not join us to God.

The mystery of the incarnation has also given the Byzantine Churches their vision of iconography. As St. John of Damascus taught, we depict Jesus in icons for He is human as we are and can be drawn in pictures. Yet we only depict Him as the incarnate Lord and, like the apostles, we bow before His glory that was revealed in the mystery of the Transfiguration on Mt. Tabor.

JESUS, FORETOLD BY JOHN

God's fragmentary revelation through the Old Testament prophets and His climactic presence in Christ are bridged in John the Baptist. In his call to repentance, John acts as an Old Testament prophet to open the hearts of God's people to receive the Messiah into their midst. As the forerunner, he points to the immediate appearance of the Messiah and introduces His ministry.

John the Baptist's significance in the Byzantine tradition is perhaps best indicated by the character and details of his presentation in iconography. As the herald or "angel" announcing the Messiah, he is sometimes depicted with two large wings, recalling the testimony of Scripture, "I send my messenger ahead of you to prepare your way before you" (Mt 11:10, quoting Mal 3:1). His right hand is shown in the gesture of preaching, and his other hand holds a scroll summarizing his preaching, often in the words, "Repent, for the kingdom of heaven is at hand" (Mt 3:2 RSV).

The physical features of John's appearance, his camel's hair garment and the barren rocks of the background, iconographically represent the wilderness. As a desert dweller, John calls to mind the exodus history of God's people, when they wandered through the barren waste. The prophets repeatedly recalled the wilderness experience as a time of special closeness to God, representative of purity of faith and zeal in devotion to Yahweh, the one true God. Going back to the wilderness became synonymous with a return to genuine faith and a renewed relationship between God and His people.

St. John the Baptist has a very prominent place in Byzantine spirituality, due to our Lord's testimony about him, "history has not known a man born of woman greater than John the Baptist" (Mt 11:11 NAB). He is ranked as the greatest of the saints, second only to the Theotokos. With her, he is represented on the icon screen and in the icon of the *Deisis* as the closest to Christ. In his role as forerunner, he is the prophet pointing to the coming of the Messiah, "Behold, the Lamb of God!" (Jn 1:36). We remember his conception (September 23), his birth (June 24), and his martyrdom by beheading (August 29). A synaxis is held in his honor because of his connection with the baptism of our Lord (January 7) and the recoveries of his relics are commemorated as well (February 24, May 25).

St. John is a model of the Christian life. He humbled himself to welcome Christ and was exalted through his humility to become the greatest of prophets. The consistent theme of his preaching was, "After me is to come a man who ranks ahead of me, because he was before me" (Jn 1:30 NAB). The contrast between Jesus and John was great. John fasted and was a model of penitence; Jesus ate and drank with sinners. Yet John saw Jesus as the One who would renew creation: "I baptize you in water for the sake of repentance, but ... He it is who will baptize you in the Holy Spirit and fire" (Mt 3:11).

JESUS, MANIFEST AT THE JORDAN

John the Baptist was only the forerunner and preacher of repentance. The kingdom and favor of God came with Jesus the Messiah. His first public manifestation took place when He was baptized by John in the Jordan. This theophany (appearance of

God) is recounted in each of the Gospels: Matthew 3:13–17; Mark 1:9–11; Luke 3:21–22 and, indirectly, John 1:31–34. When Jesus emerged from the waters, the Gospels record, the Holy Spirit descended in the form of a dove. The voice of the Father was heard from heaven, "This is my beloved Son. My favor rests on him."

Thus the moment of Jesus' baptism was an apparition of the Trinity, made manifest for our salvation. Throughout the Old Testament the mystery of Christ was beginning to be revealed and was in a certain manner already present. In light of the whole plan of salvation, we can now see that God was revealing His Word to humanity in preparation of the future Christ. More than this, we can see Christ as present in all ages. God spoke to Israel, in Him and for Him, anticipating that future which would see the fullness of salvation.

This manifestation of the Trinity is commemorated in the Church as one of its greatest feasts, the Theophany (January 6). By this theophany Jesus was revealed as the Messiah, the "Anointed One" of God, His true Son, one with the Father and equal to Him in divinity. Since the Lord Jesus was without sin, His baptism was a voluntary acceptance of the consequences of sin, so that He might raise us up from sin and make us sharers in the divine life. On this day water is solemnly consecrated to proclaim that, as Christ's incarnation enables human nature to be deified, His presence in the material creation renders matter a vehicle of holiness.

By means of liturgical celebrations such as these, the Church constantly proclaims that the events of the Lord's life are not merely happenings of the past. They represent a part of His plan of salvation which is still at work for us today and will be fulfilled in the future. The hymns for the feast shout out, "Today, Christ is baptized; He emerges from the water and uplifts the world with Him... . Today all creation is enlightened. Today all nature rejoices... . Today the nature of water is sanctified."

After His baptism, Jesus began His ministry with a period of fasting and prayer in the desert, before publicly proclaiming His message and purpose. This was the pattern for prophetic ministry, reflecting the experience of a people steeped in the meaning of exodus. In the desert Jesus was tempted, but He destroyed the power of evil by His obedience to the Father.

We continue this pattern in our own celebration of the Christian life by observing a forty day fast after the feast of Theophany and before the feast of the Resurrection. Our observance of Lent is the renewal of our baptismal promise to renounce evil forever and to follow after Christ.

JESUS, MANIFEST IN THE GOSPELS

The story of our Lord's life is told in four distinct Gospels written by four different men under the inspiration of the Spirit. In each we encounter diverse emphases and approaches, which result in different portrayals of the same events. Each of the four evangelists is rather like an artist executing a portrait of the same topic, Jesus Christ as Savior and Redeemer. Each one performed this task according to his talent and vision. Recognizing this dimension in the formation of the Gospels helps us to arrive at a more genuine understanding of its message.

Each Gospel has basic insights which are woven through the many incidents presented. Each applies certain shades or hues to the image of Christ found in them. Mark's purpose, echoing throughout his Gospel, is to demonstrate that Jesus was indeed the Christ (Messiah) who inaugurates the kingdom of God. Matthew's Gospel expands this presentation to show this Jesus as truly divine and truly human. Luke in his Gospel and his Acts of the Apostles shows the message of salvation as meant to go beyond the borders of Israel. He highlights the vast sweep of Christianity's universal mission ranging from humble beginnings in Jerusalem to a glorious fulfillment in Rome. In John's Gospel, a mystical approach constantly finds sacramental meaning in ordinary facts and events. John is imbued with the overwhelming realization that "The Word became flesh and made his dwelling among us, ... and we have seen his glory" (Jn 1:14).

Each Gospel reflects a certain perspective that is significant to its purpose as it describes Jesus' preaching, the signs and wonders He worked and His commissioning of the Apostles. Yet the style of the particular Evangelist and the manner of his presentation were applied to memories and accounts of Jesus, which were the fruit of the living Church's reflection and life. These materials were received from the Church. The Evangelists interpreted and applied the words and deeds of Jesus to provide the Church with life and instruction in all the moments of its existence. Jesus' story was not to be seen merely as a chronology of past events but as a source of ongoing power that daily challenges and directs Christians in and through their communities.

The Gospel accounts show evidence of their formation within the living context of the early Church. The miracle stories reflect this through an economy of words and the absence of irrelevant details which would detract from the saving effect of Christ's power. Memories of the sayings and acts of Jesus which were appropriate to the problems facing the early Church were incorporated into the Gospels, as the community found direction and counsel for these early crises in the Lord's words. Hence, many sayings and events are recorded in the Gospels, not only because they were a part of the life of Christ but also because they spoke to important concerns in the life of the early Church.

The evangelists do not present a photographic reproduction of Jesus' words and deeds. They sketch a portrait of the meaning behind His words and deeds as understood by the Church enlightened through the Holy Spirit. Our understanding of the Gospels and the other Scriptures, as well as the whole pattern of God's dealings with humanity, is aided when we come to appreciate this stance.

During the course of the year the Byzantine Churches read all of the four Gospels at divine services. The Gospel of St. Matthew is read from Pentecost to the feast of the Exaltation of the Holy Cross (September 14). The Gospel of St. Luke is read from then to the beginning of the Great Fast. The Gospel of St. Mark is read during the Great Fast. The weekday readings of Mark occur at the ends of the periods of Matthew and Luke. The Gospel of St. John is read during the fifty days from Pascha (Easter) to Pentecost, representing the most ancient part of the cycle.[6] Additionally, the Gospel passages recounting special events in our Lord's life are read on the annual commemorating feast. Only part of the public reading of the Gospel can be heard if attendance is limited to Sundays and Holydays.

JESUS, MANIFEST ON TABOR

One event of the Lord's life has been especially important in Byzantine theology. It is recorded in all three Synoptic Gospels (Mt 17:1–8; Mk 9:1–7; Lk 9:28–36) and is referred to in 2 Peter 1:16–19. Jesus led His chief disciples, Peter, James and John, onto a high mountain. He underwent transfiguration (in Greek, *metamorphosis*) in their sight so that "His face shone like the sun, and his garments became as radiant as light" (Mt 17:2). These are tokens of the indescribable glory in which His divinity was revealed. Here to there is a theophany of the Trinity: the voice of the Father gives the same testimony as at the baptism, "This is my beloved Son with whom I am well pleased. Listen to him" (Mt 17:5). The Spirit appears as a bright cloud overshadowing Jesus with Moses and Elijah beside Him.

The hymns of the feast in the Byzantine Churches repeatedly connect the Transfiguration with the paschal mystery. At vespers, for example, we sing, "Before Your crucifixion, O Lord, You took Your disciples upon a high mountain, that, having beheld Your wonders, they should not be afraid at Your suffering ... You were transfigured before them ... to show them the splendor of the resurrection ..." By one tradition, the Transfiguration occurred forty days before Christ's passion. Because of this tradition, the Church celebrates the feast of the Transfiguration on August 6, forty days before the feast of the Exaltation of the Cross.

The Transfiguration became important in Byzantine theology because it reveals so clearly the mission of Christ. In the Transfiguration Jesus reveals the accomplishment of God's plan in the mystery of the Incarnation. The vesper hymns of the Transfiguration proclaim, "Through Your transfiguration You returned Adam's nature to its original splendor, restoring its very elements to the glory and brilliance of Your divinity."

JESUS, THE NEW PASSOVER

In ordering their presentation of the life and teaching of Jesus, the Gospel writers were conscious of one dominant theme, the resurrection of Jesus Christ. The whole Paschal mystery, Jesus' passing through death to new life, became the key by which everything else in the Gospel could be understood. The holy light at Pentecost empowered the Apostles to preach the event of Christ's death and resurrection as the definitive moment of salvation. The fulfillment of all that was promised in God's plan of salvation came about through the death and resurrection of Christ. This same recognition of God's great deeds of salvation is celebrated by Eastern Christians in the triumphal proclamation of the Resurrection in *Pascha* (Passover), the feast of feasts. It is the source of all theology, the heart of the Christian experience of daily life.

The Resurrection revealed to the Apostles that Jesus was *Kyrios* ("Lord," linguistically equivalent to "God"). Jesus truly suffered and died on the Cross, but He rose from the dead and came back in His human body. His humanity was no longer restrained or confined in any way. He returns as a man whose godhead functions dynamically through His humanity. Jesus would

do now what could only be done by God. He would bestow the Holy Spirit, spoken of in the Old Testament as the greatest messianic gift. At His first appearance after the Resurrection, Jesus "breathed on them and said, 'Receive the Holy Spirit. If you forgive anyone's sins, they are forgiven; if you retain them, they are retained'" (Jn 20:22–23). After the descent of the Holy Spirit on Pentecost, Peter would preach, "This is the Jesus God has raised up, and we are his witnesses. Exalted at God's right hand, he first received the promised Holy Spirit from the Father, then poured this Spirit out on us. This is what you see and now hear ... Therefore, let the whole house of Israel know beyond any doubt that God has made both Lord and Messiah this Jesus whom you crucified" (Acts 2:32–33,36 NAB).

Not surprisingly, the passion of Jesus initially had to be treated in an apologetic fashion. Since pre-Christian Judaism did not expect a suffering Messiah, this aspect was problematic. The more dominant theme in the Old Testament emphasized the triumphant aspect of the Messiah, leading many to expect a political triumph. Yet the "servant of the Lord God" in Isaiah 42, 49, 51, 53 was "a man in suffering ... dishonored and not esteemed ... he was wounded on account of our sins and was bruised because of our iniquities ... and by bruises we are healed" (Is 53:3–5). The Apostles, therefore, dealt with the mystery of the passion by explaining it in two ways. First, they showed that it had been willed by God and had been a part of the whole plan of salvation. Second, they contended that Jesus was not responsible for His death, which was caused by human malice.

The experience and writing of St. Paul gives the passion a new dimension. At first frustrated and discouraged by many failures, St. Paul began to look back over his whole missionary experience from a new light. He saw that suffering and persecution had often accompanied his attempts to plant the seeds of the Gospel. However, the seed had actually grown. Paul clearly recognized in his own experience the central teaching of Isaiah the Prophet, that only in the intense awareness of one's weakness could one be filled with the power of God. St. Paul wrote, "God forbid that I ever boast of anything but the cross of our Lord Jesus Christ..." (Gal 6:14); "I will do no boasting about myself unless it be about my weaknesses..." (2 Cor 12:5); "The message of the Cross is complete absurdity to those who are headed for ruin, but to us who are experiencing salvation it is the power of God" (1 Cor 1:18). To live in this mystery means to discover the paradox of the way of Christ — wisdom and life come through weakness and death to self.

The celebration of the Death and Resurrection of our Lord is at the heart of Christian worship. Each of the sacraments in some way brings us from the death of sin into life in the Trinity through Christ and by the power of the Spirit. We celebrate this pattern of our salvation in the most solemn way during Holy Week and Bright Week (the week after Pascha). At Matins and Vespers we follow the final confrontations of Jesus and His enemies in the Gospel of St. Matthew, and the whole story of Jesus' death according to the four Gospels is told in the Matins and Royal Hours of Great Friday. On Great Friday evening the burial of Jesus is dramatically reenacted by the procession with the burial shroud, a cloth upon which is depicted an icon of the body of our Lord taken from the cross. Pascha, the feast of feasts, is welcomed with a procession moving from the empty tomb to the radiance of the illumined church. The resurrection of Christ is then proclaimed by the magnificent troparion, "Christ is risen from the dead, by death He conquered death, and to those in the graves He granted life," followed by the whole Resurrection Canon.

The great feast of Pascha is extended throughout fifty days. On the eighth day of the feast, we remember Christ's appearance to the apostle Thomas. On the second Sunday after Pascha, the Gospel of the Resurrection according to Mark is read; and the memory of the women who came to the tomb with gifts of ointment is celebrated. On the twenty-fifth day we recall the promise Jesus made in the Temple to give us the gift of the Holy Spirit. This *Mid-Pentecost* connects the two celebrations: the mystery of the Resurrection and the giving of the Holy Spirit.

The Feast of Ascension commemorates the return of Jesus to the glory of His Father, the present mystery in which Christ now sits at the right hand of the Father as High Priest and Savior. At the Ascension, we see the humanity of Jesus enthroned with the Father, just as we saw the divinity of Jesus revealed through His body at the Transfiguration. The fifty days close with the solemnity of Pentecost, proclaiming the coming of the Holy Spirit, whom our

Lord promised would be our Paraclete (comforter and advocate) forever.

The work of Christ — His message, life, death and resurrection — has initiated the new and final age, the "fullness of time." Sin and death have been dealt a decisive blow by virtue of the saving power of Christ, but they still exist in the present age as the final phase of salvation history unfolds. We look for the outcome of the vast design originating with the call of God to Abraham and culminating in a new world whose age is yet to come. We can indeed speak of this new age as being already present in the very heart of the events, in the constant march of history. By His resurrection, Christ reestablished creation, having already restored all humanity. Yet from now to the final consummation of all things, this reality is not entirely evident. It must be discovered in the very person of Jesus and, with the bestowal of the Spirit, in the life and mysteries of the Church.

For the moment this "new world," through which the Spirit penetrates all of reality, exists fully only in its first fruits, the Body of Christ. At the end of time, it will be revealed fully in a "new heaven and a new earth" (Rv 21:1). In the meantime this glorious body of Christ, conqueror of sin and death, is indeed real but beyond our sense perception. The question is not one of asking "where is Christ?" nor of imagining Him as far off. This new age, in which Christ reigns and for which we must wait, is not outside our present world. Instead it transcends it from within. For the moment it is inaccessible to our senses and imagination, but it is no less real. We must reach out to it through the perception of faith and the economy of the sacraments, particularly the Eucharist. We might say that the fullness of time is now, but not yet.

THE FUTURE KINGDOM

The Lord Jesus preached constantly about the Kingdom of God or the Kingdom of heaven and announced that it was "at hand." We pray in the Divine Liturgy with the assurance of its present reality: "You brought us to heaven and bestowed upon us Your future kingdom" (anaphora). To understand this kingdom, we must not let our preconceptions blind our understanding. Since monarchies are no longer a common form of government, we no longer have direct experience of what a king is.

Christ was quite clear that His Kingdom differed from the governments of the world (Jn 18:36). God is a king by analogy. More precisely, all human authority is only a reflection of God's authority. Sometimes the disciples misunderstood the kingdom as a permanent political dynasty that the Messiah would establish here on earth to bring eternal peace by gathering all people under God's sovereignty. Christ rejected the notion of a kingdom established by force. He left all people free either to choose Him or to reject Him, and to receive the consequences of that decision.

The Kingdom of God "does not belong to this world" (Jn 19:36). It is a return to the ancient concept that the Lord alone is the king of all. As Creator and Lover of Mankind, He alone has absolute authority, which He exercises only in relation to the absolute gift of freedom that He has given us. Earthly kings may lord it over others, but in God all people are equal. All must serve each other according to the gift given them (cf. 1 Cor 12).

The reign of God is not to be thought of in terms of power and might but of enlightenment, righteousness and love. His kingdom is the promised land where the Holy Spirit guides the heart of every person, as we sing at Pentecost, "Your good Spirit shall lead me into the land of righteousness!" (Ps 142/143:10). The secular world today often sees holiness and righteousness as character weaknesses. The Gospel sees them as the principal characteristics of God's people and as a hope that justice can prevail. As Jesus promised, "Blessed are the lowly; they shall inherit the land. Blessed are they who hunger and thirst for holiness; they shall have their fill" (Mt 5:5–6).

The Kingdom of God is at the very heart of Jesus' Gospel. His first preaching is recorded as "Reform your lives! The kingdom of heaven is at hand" (Mt 4:17). The Divine Liturgy begins, "Blessed is the Kingdom of the Father, and of the Son and of the Holy Spirit." However, revelation seems to indicate sometimes that the kingdom is imminent and at other times that it is in the future. In Jesus' preaching, the kingdom seems imminent, "I assure you, among those standing here there are some who will not experience death before they see the Son of Man come in his kingship" (Mt 16:28). The Gospel of St. Luke in a difficult passage says, "Neither is it a matter of reporting that it is 'here' or 'there.' The kingdom of God is already in your midst" (17:21).

On the other hand, the fullness of the kingdom of God seemingly must await some indeterminate future. Therefore, we pray daily in the Lord's Prayer, "Thy kingdom come." At the Last Supper Jesus told His disciples, "I will not drink this fruit of the vine from now until the day when I drink it new with you in my Father's reign" (Mt 26:29), and "as for the exact day or hour, no one knows it, not even the angels in heaven, but the Father only" (Mt 24:36).

THE SPIRIT AS FIRST PLEDGE

Before His ascension into glory, the Lord promised, "know that I am with you always, until the end of the world!" (Mt 28:20). Jesus explained, "I will ask the Father and he will give you another Paraclete to be with you always, the Spirit of truth ... He remains with you and will be within you. I will not leave you orphaned; I will come back to you" (Jn 14:16–18).

The inheritance that our Lord left us after His death, resurrection, and return to glory is the gift of the Holy Spirit. St. Paul writes, "In [Christ] you were chosen; when you heard the glad tidings of salvation, the word of truth, and believed in it, you were sealed with the Holy Spirit, who had been promised. He is the pledge of our inheritance, the first payment against the full redemption of a people God had made his own, to praise his glory" (Eph 1:13–14). The Holy Spirit, given to us in baptism-chrismation, is our assurance of salvation and sanctification. Through Him God's promises begin to be fulfilled, and in Him we are being brought to perfection. As St. Paul writes, "God is the one who firmly establishes us along with you in Christ; it is he who anointed us and has sealed us, thereby depositing the first payment, the Spirit, in our hearts" (2 Cor 1:21–22).

The Gospel points to the reality that Christ Himself is the kingdom.[7] Now, in the age of the Church, we may make the equally valid point that the Kingdom is equally the Spirit as it is Christ. St. Simeon the New Theologian identifies the Kingdom with the Spirit:

> The "kingdom of heaven" consists in partaking of the Holy Spirit, for this is what the saying "The kingdom of heaven is within you" (Lk 17:21) means. So we must endeavor to receive the Holy Spirit within ourselves and to keep Him."[8]

The Spirit mediates the presence of God in the present age, the era of the Church. He actively leads and guides the Church and individual believers. By His power, Christ comes among us in the holy mysteries. Through the Holy Spirit, we become a priestly people, able to offer the "sacrifice of praise" and to be formed into the living temple of God. "The proof that you are sons is the fact that God has sent forth into our hearts the spirit of His Son which cries out, 'Abba!' ('Father!')" (Gal 4:6).

The kingdom of God is fully present in Jesus the Messiah, but it will yet be fulfilled for us. Until that time of fruition, the Spirit at work in us and among us is the great sign of our salvation. Likewise, the gift of the Spirit is simultaneously the complete pouring out of divine life into us but is also the pledge of what shall yet be. As St. Paul said, "we ourselves, though we have the Spirit as first fruits, groan inwardly while we await the redemption of our bodies" (Rom 8:23).

OUR HOPE OF RESURRECTION

Nicholas Cabasilas tell us that "the life in Christ originates in this life and arises from it. It is perfected, however, in the life to come, when we shall have reached that last day."[9] This end of human history will be signaled by Christ's return in glory, known as the second coming or *parousia*. It is predicted many times in the New Testament (e.g. Mt 24–25). At His return, this masterpiece of God's handiwork, the plan of salvation, will be complete. The Lord Jesus will reveal fully the sons and daughters of God. Their bodies will be freed from that corruption to which they are now enslaved, and they will enter into the new world of the Spirit. The resurrection of the body will crown the drama of salvation in which God will be all in all (Rom 8:19–25; 1 Cor 15:22–28; Rv 21).

Speculation about the last things has always had a certain attraction for some Christians. Throughout the centuries, especially in times of upheaval, the prophetic passages have sometimes been read literally and applied to particular institutions and people. We must resist the temptation to allow our own guesses about the future to be read back into Scripture and used to judge others. Jesus himself said, "as for the exact day or hour, no one knows it, neither the angels in heaven nor the Son, but the Father only" (Mt 24:36). St. Paul also cautions us about forming concepts regarding the 'how' of the after-life. He told the Corinthians, "Perhaps someone will say, 'How are the dead to be raised up? What kind of body will the have?' A nonsensical question!" (1 Cor 15:35–36).

Our hope for the future is founded on the resurrection of Christ (1 Cor 15:12–19). After His resurrection Christ appeared to His followers as truly flesh and blood, yet gloriously transformed. He came and went mysteriously. Locked doors were no barrier to Him. To some He appeared "in another form" (Mk 16:12) and was recognized only in the breaking of bread. This resurrection is our hope and the goal of *theosis* (Greek for "deification" or "becoming like God"). St. Paul wrote, "Death came through a man [Adam]; hence the resurrection of the dead comes through a man also" (1 Cor 15:21). He also adds that in our resurrection we will be transformed as Christ was. "So it is with the resurrection of the dead. What is sown in the earth is subject to decay, what rises is incorruptible. What is sown is ignoble, what rises is glorious. Weakness is sown, strength rises up" (1 Cor 15:42–43).

The exact nature of our resurrection is unknown to us in the present, for "eye has not seen, ear has not heard, nor has it so much as dawned on man, what God has prepared for those who love him" (1 Cor 2:9). Yet, we know that God respects our nature as both physical and spiritual creatures. By becoming human, Christ showed the importance of our body. By His glorification in the transfiguration and resurrection, He revealed that the body, too, has a share in the future destiny of the person. As a result we can say with confidence, "I expect the resurrection of the dead, and the life of the world to come: (Nicene-Constantinopolitan Creed).

"TO JUDGE THE LIVING AND THE DEAD"

We know something about one further aspect of the future life: the judgment of deeds. God is portrayed in Scripture as a judge, because all creation falls under His dominion and providence. The final judgment is a sign that He is committed to rightly ordering His creation. This judgment affects each individual person, as St. Paul clearly taught, "The lives of all of us are to be revealed before the tribunal of Christ so that each one may receive his recompense, good or bad, according to his life in the body" (2 Cor 5:10). In Christ's parable of the separation of the sheep from the goats we see that even those who do not know Him will be judged (Mt 25:31–46). Here charity "to the least of my brethren" is the principal basis on which humanity will be tested.

60

THE PREPARED THRONE

This judgment of the individual person results in everlasting life with God for those who have lived in a godly way; for those who have failed, eternal suffering is in store. In the concrete language of the Scriptures, the state of eternal salvation is termed "heaven"; eternal condemnation is described as "hell." Heaven is a Holy City, the New Jerusalem (Rv 21–22), while hell is *Gehenna,* the Valley of Hennom,[10] which served as the garbage dump of Jerusalem and burned continually (Mk 9:43). The Scriptures use such images because what they speak of is indescribable: the fullness or absence of life.

The essence of heaven is union with God, in whom we find our perfection. Being made in God's image, we attain salvation in becoming as much like God as possible. Though we can never know God as He is in Himself, we can come continually closer to Him who deifies us. The future kingdom is the fulfillment of our destiny as humanity and as individuals. In it we are perfected by constant growth in union, knowledge and love of God.

Comparably, the most terrible aspect of hell is eternal separation from God, the Creator and Lover of Mankind, in whom we could have found our perfection. No torment could be any greater than this loss. Jesus used the image of Gehenna to describe the state of those who were condemned, for it combined the ideas of rejection and of punishment. He called it the "everlasting fire prepared for the devil and his angels" (Mt 25:41), and the "fiery furnace where there is wailing and the gnashing of teeth" (Mt 13:42), a sign of despair.

The possibility of salvation also implies the possibility of failure or condemnation. God created us in His image and likeness as free beings with autonomy of action and that carries with it the risk of failure. Our freedom is real, and the consequences of our free choices are likewise real. Union with God always remains a possibility as long as we have free will.

Non-believers regard the hope of heaven as mere wishful thinking, unsupported by evidence. The rationality of our hope is seen in the love of God for us in the Cross and Resurrection. Is belief in heaven as the fulfillment of our existence any more difficult to accept than the wondrous fact that we exist at all, or that we are capable of knowing truth and good?

In the same way the idea of hell has been criticized both from within and from without the Church. From within, some have said that a merciful God could not condemn people to an eternal hell. In the third century Origen held this view and was censured for this opinion by the Church. From without, non-believers claim that the Church uses the idea of hell only to take away freedom and to burden us with the threat of eternal terror after death.

In the Tradition, however, the images of heaven and hell point to more than individual reward or punishment; they refer to the ultimate transformation of the whole world. All of creation as well as individual persons will be transfigured in glory. "Then I saw a new heavens and a new earth. The former heavens and the former earth had passed away, and the sea was no longer" (Rv 21:1). The "sea" here may represent the dark and dangerous forces causing human death. Hell is an important aspect of that transformation: the ultimate destruction of sin. St. John of Damascus calls it a kind of baptism: one in which we encounter the destructive power of a flood. "The eighth [baptism] is the last, which is not saving, but which destroys evil: for evil and sin no longer have sway: yet it punishes without end."[11]

The Church teaches that in Christ we received the fullness of the revelation of God. Through faith in the Lord Jesus, we are reconciled to the Father; the sin of our first father and mother is erased; and we become sharers in the life of the Trinity. God becomes truly "our Father" (Mt 6:9), and His kingdom is coming to be in power among us. Our prayer of faith is that it may actually reach its fulfillment through the free acceptance of all people, "Thy kingdom come!" (Mt 6:10). We can see a tension between faith and hope. In faith the kingdom has already come in Christ, who "conquered death by His death" and is risen from the dead. In hope though, "we are God's children now; what we shall later be has not yet come to light. We know that when it comes to light we shall be like him, for we shall see him as he is" (1 Jn 3:2).

The human race will someday end because we are creatures incarnate in time, which itself must end. For the non-believer nothing exists beyond the end. Because of our faith in Christ, however, we believe that in the end God will "bring all things in the heavens and on earth into one under Christ's headship" (Eph 1:10). Christians hope in the *parousia* as fulfillment of His plan for humanity. Thus, a common prayer of the early Christians was "Come, Lord" *(Marana, tha)*. It remains so in the Church's liturgy: "Every time, then, you eat this bread and drink this cup, you proclaim the death of the Lord until He comes" (1 Cor 11:26). The hope of the future kingdom is so firmly rooted in the Gospels and the apostolic writings that it became one of the central articles of faith in the Creed: "I believe in one Lord Jesus Christ, [who] shall come again with glory, to judge the living and the dead, and of His kingdom there shall be no end... . I expect the resurrection of the dead; and the life of the world to come" (Nicene-Constantinopolitan Creed).

PRAYER FOR THE DEAD

"Death will be swallowed up in victory" (1 Cor 15:54). We sing of the risen Christ, "by death He conquered Death" (Paschal Troparion). The solidarity of the human race extends beyond death to life. Our prayers help those who have died and we are joined to them by their intercession.[12] One of the most ancient prayers for the dead, which concludes the litany for the departed, asks God, "give rest to the soul of Your departed servants (name), in a place of light, a place of refreshment, a place of repose, where there is no pain, sorrow or sighing... . Forgive every sin committed by them, in word or deed or thought, for there is no one who lives and who does not sin." Those who have achieved union with God may also help us by their prayers. This teaching, called the "communion of saints", is a positive affirmation that even death cannot destroy the bonds of Christian love we have for one another in the Lord.

3 — The Mystery Shared

In the Old Testament the "Church" was the people chosen by God and gathered into His presence. The Hebrew word for this chosen people was *qahal* (in Greek, *ecclesia) yahweh,* meaning "the assembly of God." The focus of this assembly was the central shrine of Israel, God's dwelling on earth, where His presence was particularly located: originally the tabernacle in the desert and later the temple of Jerusalem.

In the New Testament, the temple of God's presence was interiorized. St. Paul taught, "Are you not aware that you are the temple of God, and that the Spirit of God dwells in you? If anyone destroys God's temple, God will destroy him. For the temple of God is holy and you are that temple" (1 Cor 3:16–17). The original meaning is lost a little in the English because the Greek word for "you" is the plural collective form, meaning the people as a group who make up the Church. St. Peter also compares the Church to a temple of stones, "You too are living stones, built as an edifice of spirit, into a holy priesthood, offering spiritual sacrifices acceptable to God through Jesus Christ" (1 Pt 2:5). There is an essential unity here: the Church is built of living people; God is present among these people both in each individual and in the assembled community.

Unity is the keynote of the Church, in which we are joined with one another in the body of Christ (cf. 1 Cor 12:12). This answers the prayer of Christ that we might be one, as He and the Father are one (Jn 17:10). In the Church we are also united with God. Because the Word of God became a human being, we become the brothers and sisters of God, for "He who consecrated and those who are consecrated are of the same nature" (Heb 2:11). All these works are accomplished through the Spirit, who "is present everywhere and fills all things" (Hymn, "O Heavenly King").

IMAGES OF THE CHURCH

The Church expresses its thoughts on its own identity chiefly through imagery. In the various idea-pictures of the Tradition, the Church seeks to make concrete its experience of union with God. A few of the most significant images are:

- *Icon of the Trinity* — The unity of the Church is built on a solid foundation: the unity of God in the Holy Trinity. The Church is the historical expression of the work of the Trinity, and its life mirrors the life of God. Hence, our vision of the Church is closely connected to what we know of the mysteries of the Trinity. The Church is an *icon* of the Trinity and in a very real sense mirrors and reflects the life of the Father, the Son, and the Holy Spirit. The Church functions, "led by the Spirit ... to make God the Father and His incarnate Son presentans in a sense visible, while ceaselessly renewing and purifying herself under the guidance of the Holy Spirit" (*Church in the Modern World*, 21). The Second Vatican Council taught, "The universal Church is seen to be 'a people brought into unity from the unity of the Father, the Son and the Holy Spirit'" (*Constitution on the Church*, 4).

The Church must show the world the meaning of living in relationship, one person to another, as the Three Persons in God live in each other. The Church does not exist except as a *group* of people united in their belief in Christ, for "where two or three are gathered in my name, there am I in their midst" (Mt 18:20). Just as the identity of the Father, the Son and the Holy Spirit comes from the relationship each has with the others, so the identity of the members of the Church flows from the rela- tionship of love which generates life and produces good works. In doing so, they present the Church as an image of the Trinity.

Western culture in modern times has rightly emphasized the value of the individual. Unfortunately, this emphasis has often minimized or eliminated an appreciation of community. People often choose to belong to a church because of its contribution to their interior life of piety: they "get something out of it." They have little thought of commitment to the other people belonging to that church. In a world which is often hostile to religion, we must be able to reflect the basic oneness of the Church by recognizing and supporting our brothers and sisters in faith. Our inner lives of faith cannot flourish in isolation from the community. Some people might dream of educating their children in Christianity and of practicing the faith outside of the institutional Church, but they will lose all knowledge and tradition within two generations. The inner life of the Church acts in the hearts of persons, but transcends individuals.

- *The Body of Christ* — Jesus Christ, the Incarnate Word, is the visible expression of the inner, loving life of God; and the visible Church is, likewise, the expression of the enduring presence of our Lord. St. Paul repeatedly speaks of the Church as the "body" of Christ in which the individual members have different roles, just as the individual parts of a human body have different roles or functions in contributing to the life of the entire body (1 Cor 12:12–27; Eph 1:22–23; 4:15–16; 5:23; Col 1:18; 2:19; Rom 12:4). The image of the Church as body underlines the unity of its members with God and each other through Christ, who is called "reconciliation" (2 Cor 5:19). St. Paul specifically identifies the Church with the Body of Christ (Eph 1:23). Through the Church we become Christ, yet we retain our own identity, in that Christ is the "head" of the Church. In his *Mystagogy*, St. Maximus the Confessor showed this identification to be one of the key points of the theology of the Fathers:

> "All are born into the Church and through it are reborn and recreated in the Spirit.... through it absolutely no one at all is in himself separated from the community since everyone

converges with all the rest and joins together with them by the one, simple and indivisible grace and power of faith. Thus to be and to appear as one body formed of different members is worthy of Christ himself, our true head.... the holy Church is an image of God because it realizes the same union of the faithful with God."[1]

• *Community of the Holy Spirit* — If Christ is the head of the Church, then, in an allegorical way, its "soul" is the Holy Spirit, the "Spirit of truth" promised by Christ (Jn 14:16–17; 16:13; Acts 1:8). The Spirit confers holiness on individual believers (1 Cor 3:15; 6:19), makes them adopted children and heirs of God (Gal 4:6; Rom 8:15–17), guides them into the truth (Jn 16:13), bestows the gifts of service which build up the Body of Christ (Eph 4:11–13), and dynamically unifies all the various members into one Body (1 Cor 12:13). Since there is but one Spirit, all the members of Christ's Body are one in God and one with each other. The Church, in other words, is a sacrament of unity, called to make the unity which it signifies really present in the world and to demonstrate that it is truly a community of the Holy Spirit.

THE CHURCH REALIZED IN THE EUCHARIST

The process of becoming God's dwelling place in the Spirit, the Body of Christ, is realized most fully in the Eucharist. Jesus compared the Kingdom of God to a banquet (Mt 22:1–14; Lk 14:16–24). At the Last Supper He revealed that the Eucharist is both the memorial of His presence and a pledge of the future banquet (Mt 26:29; Mk 14:25; Lk 22:18; 1 Cor 11:26). Jesus chose this meal as one of the last things He would do with His disciples. Having come to form a new order in the world, He established a sign to remember and continue His work. The Eucharist provides for those who partake of it both nourishment and a sense of common unity through the natural significance of a meal taken together as a family or a community.

The way we use bread in the Divine Liturgy signifies the unity of the Church. The Eucharistic Bread, called the "Lamb," — Christ, the "Lamb of God who takes away the sin of the world" — rests on the diskos, surrounded by smaller particles representing the Theotokos, the angels and saints, and those for whom we pray. This arrangement symbolizes the entire Church, the Body of Christ, who offers and is offered. After the Lord's Prayer the Lamb is broken into four parts for distribution to the communicants. This acts out in ritual what St. Paul taught, "is not the bread we break a sharing in the body of Christ? Because the loaf of bread is one, we, many though we are, are one body, for we all partake of the one loaf" (1 Cor 10:16–17).

The Eucharist builds the Church. St. Paul calls both the Eucharist and the Church the Body of Christ. One is not possible without the other. In the Divine Liturgy, the bread and wine, which are offered "in all and for all," become the body and blood of Christ. Just as the bread and wine are changed into the body and blood of Christ through the power of the Holy Spirit, so too the entire Church, and ultimately the whole world, is transformed into the image and likeness of God through the celebration of the Eucharist. The Church is the visible sign of God's continuing presence and activity in the world, and it is never more itself than when it calls forth the presence of Christ under the visible signs of the Eucharist.

The Second Vatican Council recognized the essential unity that exists between the Church and the Eucharist, a theme so much at the heart of Eastern thought. In its *Decree on the Ministry and Life of Priests*, it refers to the Eucharist as "the very heartbeat of the congregation of the faithful" (No. 5), and says that "no Christian community ...can be built up unless it has its basis and center in the celebration of the most Holy Eucharist" (No. 6). The Eucharist is "the source of perfecting the Church" (*Decree on the Missionary Activity of the Church*, 39), the means whereby "the unity of the Church is both signified and brought about" (*Decree on Ecumenism*, 2).

MISSION OF THE CHURCH

The Eucharist is a sign of Christ's love and self-sacrifice for others. The Church continues to manifest this love, to do good within and beyond itself. All the faithful, as its members, must act in the same way. The Church lives out the love of God which creates and redeems. On the individual level, acting out of love can form personality in others and lift them up from failure. On the community level, it can begin to bring about God's kingdom on earth. Like the apostles, the Church is sent on a mission involving four basic actions, called in the Greek language of the New Testament: *kerygma, leitourgia, koinonia,* and *diakonia.*

- *Kerygma* — Kerygma originally meant the proclamation of a herald or messenger. In the early Church, it came to mean the first preaching of the mystery of Jesus. The early Christians, living in a world ignorant of Christ, were acutely conscious of their mandate to proclaim Christ and to preach the good news of salvation. Just before He ascended to the Father, Jesus commanded His followers to "make disciples of all nations, teaching them to carry out everything I have commanded you" (Mt 28:19–20). He told them, "you are to be my witnesses in Jerusalem, throughout Judea and Samaria, yes even to the ends of the earth" (Acts 1:8).

  Christians have the duty of being witnesses (*martyres*) to the Gospel of Christ. We may proclaim it directly by words, but we also affirm it by our way of life. Bearing witness means more than teaching. It includes a personal involvement in the message that is being proclaimed. The Gospel is not a mere recitation of facts; it is the proclamation of an event which actively involves the listener. Jesus heals, forgives, raises and teaches us as surely as He did the original hearers. The teaching of the Church is not a collection of stories from the past, but a living tradition that challenges us to an active faith of mercy and justice. Hence, the writings of the apostles and evangelists are read at every Liturgy and the Gospel Book is treated with great honor. Having heard the kerygma in our hearts, our response becomes like Peter's, "Lord, to whom shall we go? You have the words of eternal life. We have come to believe; we are convinced that you are God's holy one" (Jn 6:68-69).

- *Leitourgia.* — The Church particularly fulfills her mission in the celebration of the divine services. Just as bearing witness means more than teaching, worship means more than performing ritual. It may be defined as the public celebration of the Church in which we singly and as a community offer ourselves to God (Rom 12:1–3). It involves ritual actions, but goes beyond outward signs to become a true "sacrifice of praise" realized by the working of the Holy Spirit (Rom 8:26).

"Liturgy" comes from two Greek words: *laos* (people) and *ergon* (work). In classical Greek it signified a public work undertaken by a citizen for the good of the community, often including a public celebration. Applying the term *Leitourgia* most particularly to the Eucharist aptly expressed the identity between Christ's work of salvation and the Church's celebration of that work. Here the commemoration of the death and resurrection of our Lord frees us from sin and at the same time makes Him and His saving work present. By the Liturgy the Church's members are brought into union with God and made holy through the action of the Spirit. By this process a people is formed and the Body of Christ is built up (1 Pt 2:5).

- *Koinonia.* — Before the eucharistic prayer, the priest blesses the people with the words, "The grace of our Lord Jesus Christ, the love of God the Father, and the communion (*koinonia*) in the Holy Spirit, be with all of you" (2 Cor 13:13). The primary meaning of *koinonia* is fellowship or communion in the Lord. It is an essential characteristic of the Church and the mission of Jesus, who prayed, "that all may be one as You, Father, are in me, and I in You" (Jn 17:21). Fellowship with Christ includes sharing in His body and blood (1 Cor 10:16–17) and in His passion and resurrection (Phil 3:10; Heb 3:14; 1 Pt 4:13). It also includes a communion in the one life of faith (Ti 1:4; 1 Jn 1:3,7), in the divine nature (2 Pt 1:4), and in the Holy Spirit (2 Cor 13:13; Phil 2:1; Heb 6:4).

  Such fellowship or communion is the chief effect of the Divine Liturgy. The Father is asked to sanctify and transform the gifts "for the communion in Your Holy Spirit." We pray that the relationships we have in the Body of Christ — both with God and with each other — be deepened through our sharing in the holy mysteries.

- *Diakonia.* — The final note of the mission of the Church is *diakonia,* which is service or ministry. Jesus' life was essentially a life of service: "the Son of Man has not come to be served but to serve — to give his life in ransom for the many" (Mk 10:45). At the Last Supper Jesus emphasized this role by washing the feet of His disciples. He told them that He, as "Teacher and Lord," was performing the task of a servant and they must do likewise (Jn 13:12–17). Led by the Lord's example, the Church established its principal ministries: the service of prayer and preaching and the service of Christian charity (cf Acts 6:1–4).

The service of Christian charity includes works which contribute to the material or spiritual well-being of others. Such works include almsgiving, hospitality, admonishing, cheering, supporting, being patient (Acts 11:29; Rom 12:6, 15, 23, 31; 2 Cor 8:4, 19f; 9:1, 12f; 1 Thes 5:12, 14). The works of charity are a consequence of the Eucharist, a distinguishing characteristic of the Church, and a sign of Christ's own mission (Mt 11:4-5). They contribute to the realization of the Kingdom of God, the new heavens and the new earth promised to Christ's followers.

THE GIFTS OF THE SPIRIT

Baptism admits the Christian into the life of the Trinity. It also makes a person a member of the Church. These two passages — the first from the limitations of our natural life into the divine life, and the second from selfish individuality into the Body of Christ, which is the Church (Col 1:18) — are inseparable. Authentic Christian faith and participation in the divine life presume membership in the Church and participation in a believing community. Life in the Trinity is real. We have truly become children of the Father; Christ is our brother; the Spirit fills our lives. This makes a real difference in how we live and act and in how we relate to others.

The Lord Jesus promised the Spirit to His followers (Jn 15:16–17, 26; 16:4–16). The Gospel writers describe the fulfillment of this promise in different ways. St. Matthew speaks of baptism in the "Father, the Son and the Holy Spirit" (28:19). St. John tells of Jesus appearing after His Resurrection and breathing the Spirit into His disciples with the gift of authority over sin (Jn 20:22–23). St. Luke tells the story of the fiftieth day, when the Holy Spirit came upon the first Christian community in the form of tongues of fire (recalling the Old Testament theophanies) and enabled the apostles to be understood in a variety of languages (Acts 2:1–12). He describes the amazement of the hearers, "How is it that each of us hears them in his native tongue? We are Parthians, Medes and Elamites. We live in Mesopotamia, Judea and Cappadocia, Pontus, the province of Asia, Phrygia, and Pamphylia, Egypt, and the regions of Libya around Cyrene" (Acts 2:8–9). From this beginning the Spirit is shown granting to His people a multiplicity of gifts according to their needs, for He loves and wishes the salvation of each and all.

"Every good gift is of the Holy Spirit, in whom all creation lives and moves" (First Antiphon of Sunday Matins, Tone Three). It is through the Holy Spirit that we receive the gifts common to all believers: confidence in the Father (Rom 8:15–16), faith in Christ (1 Cor 12:3), and the very ability "to pray as we should" (Rom 8:26). Following the Spirit's lead in daily life produces "love, joy, patient endurance, kindness, generosity, faith, mildness and chastity" (Gal 5:22).

The apostolic tradition affirms that each believer is called to be a temple of the Spirit. This is why the newly baptized receive the gift of the Spirit in the mystery of *chrismation*. In this sacrament the believer is anointed with myron (olive oil mixed with many fragrances) on several parts of the body. The multitude of fragrances symbolizes the variety of gifts of the Spirit, and the different anointings symbolize that the faithful Christian receives the Spirit for all the needs of life. St. Simeon of Thessalonica remarked that in this mystery the baptized and chrismated person received all the divine gifts, except holy priesthood (*On the Holy Mysteries* 66, PG 155, 229). Thus the whole Church is built up by this diversity of gifts which are received by the new member of the Body of

Christ. Through these gifts of the Holy Spirit, the individual person is joined uniquely to the Body as an integral part to assist in its growth and perfection.

The Church calls upon the Spirit at the beginning of every liturgical service. With the hymn, "O heavenly King", we ask the Spirit who prays in us (cf Rom 8:26) to be with us as we gather in the Lord's name. The presence and operation of the Spirit in the Church's worship serve to join it to Christ's own worship of the Father.

It is particularly in the Divine Liturgy that the gift of the Holy Spirit given in baptism and chrismation is renewed. At the epiclesis we invoke the Father to send the Spirit anew upon us and upon our offering. St. John Chrysostom describes it as, "The priest stands, bringing down not fire, but the Holy Spirit: and he offers prayer at length, not that a fire may be kindled and destroy the offering (cf. 1 Kgs/1 Sm 18:34–39), but that grace may fall upon the sacrifice through that prayer, and kindle the souls of all" (*On the Priesthood* 6.4). The Spirit is truly present in the Church in the Liturgy, "presiding and purifying offenses, God and deifier, fire proceeding from fire, speaking, active, distributor of gifts" (sticheron at the praises, Pentecost Matins). We affirm this as after Communion we sing the Pentecost hymn, "we have received the heavenly Spirit." Through the Holy Spirit working in the Liturgy the Church is built up as "living stones, built as an edifice of spirit, into a holy priesthood, offering spiritual sacrifices acceptable to God through Jesus Christ" (1 Pt 2:5).

TRADITION, WORK OF THE HOLY SPIRIT

One of the most important gifts of the Spirit is *Holy Tradition*. Authentic Tradition is the life of God given to the Church by the revelation of our Lord Jesus Christ. It has been described as "like a mirror, in which the Church, during its pilgrim journey here on earth, contemplates God, from whom she receives everything, until such time as she is brought to see him face to face as he really is (cf. 1 Jn 3:2)" (*Dogmatic Constitution on Divine Revelation*, 7). Living Tradition is the way that the Church accepts and expresses the life given to it by our Lord Jesus Christ. It cannot be reduced to a certain number of facts or sayings, but is the acceptance and perception of the whole reality that underlies all the faith.

Most Protestant commmunities hold to only one deposit of the truths of faith, the Bible. For the historic Churches, however, revelation is seen as more than a collection of practices, sayings and facts that are contained in the Bible. It is rather the totality of life in Christ witnessed to by apostolic writers and fathers of the Church, which amplifies and focuses written Scripture through the life and understanding of the people of God. Sacred Scripture was not written in a timeless vacuum nor is the Holy Spirit limited to the pages of Scripture. The same Spirit who inspired the apostolic writers has also been at work in the Fathers of the Church, the formative Councils, the divine services, the icons and the experience of the saints forming a continuity of life and faith with the early Church.

In popular speech, certain practices and sayings are often called "traditions." These customs may or may not be elements of *the* Tradition itself, which is "the self-identity of the Church through the ages and is the organic and visible expression of the Life of the Spirit in the Church,"[2] A specific practice could be an element of the Tradition if it is a reflection of the divine life in the Body of Christ. Thus the practice of iconography, which proclaims both the incarnation and the work of the Holy Spirit in the lives of the saints, is an element of the Tradition.

Certain customs may be expressions of a Tradition in varying degrees. Fasting itself is a practice witnessed to by Christ Himself. Fasting on Wednesdays and Fridays is an apostolic expression of this Tradition. Other fasts, practiced by different local Churches at different times, are also meaningful expressions of this

Tradition, but of a lesser degree. Fasting out of personal or sectarian pride is actually a denial of the Tradition. The Lord was aware of the dangers of this kind of tradition when He admonished the Pharisees not, "... to disregard God's commandment and cling to what is human tradition" (Mk 7:8).

Tradition is transmitted or "handed over" by one group of persons to another, by one generation to another. It is expressed in the following outward forms or elements, all of which reveal something of God's life to us.

- *The Scriptures* — The single source of revelation is God Himself: "In times past, God spoke in fragmentary and varied ways to our fathers through the prophets; in this, the final age, he has spoken to us through his Son" (Heb 1:1-2). Revelation comes down to us expressed in a number of forms and elements. The Scriptures may be described as the foremost written element of the Tradition.

  The Church understands the Scriptures to have been written by a number of individuals, known and unknown, through the inspiration of the Holy Spirit and to have been accepted by the Church over a sometimes lengthy period, also through the inspiration of the Holy Spirit. Thus, most of the New Testament books were written between the years 50 and 100 A.D., but it would be over 200 years before there was a univerally accepted "canon", or list of Scriptures recognized by all the Churches as being truly inspired by God. Once acknowledged as such, the canon of Scripture became normative for the Church.

  These holy writings, called the New Testament, have a special place in the life of the Church. They are recommended to all the faithful as the first source of our knowledge about Christ and His teachings. They stand before the Church as a constant call to be faithful to the kingdom and vision proclaimed by our Lord. In each Divine Liturgy, a selection from one of the New Testament Epistles or the Acts of the

Apostles is read, followed by a reading from one of the four Gospels. The book containing the Gospels is richly bound and carried in procession. The reading of the Gospel is carried out with a solemnity appropriate to the Word of God. The homily or sermon, a crucial part of the celebration of the Liturgy, is intended to be a living explanation of the meaning of these Scriptures for the congregation present.

Many Christians today call themselves Biblical literalists, "fundamentalists" or "Bible-believing Christians". Generally they hold that the Bible must be read according to the exact literal meaning of its words and never colored by the circumstances of these works and their literary genres. The Catholic Church, however, teaches that the way people today understand an ancient writing may not even be what the human author directly intended. For proper understanding of the Scriptures, "due attention must be paid both to the customary and characteristic patterns of perception, speech and narrative which prevailed at the time of the sacred writer, and to the conventions which the people of his time followed in their dealings with one another" *(Dogmatic Constitution on Divine Revelation*, 12). Since the words of God are written in the words of human beings, they must be understood in the context of the writers' intentions and circumstances. God inspired men to write; He did not violate their free will by taking over their bodies and making their hands write specific words. Scripture is like the mystery of the Incarnation, for "the words of God, expressed in human words, are in every way like human language, just as the Word of the eternal Father, when he took on himself the flesh of human weakness, became like men" *(Ibid.*, 13). Sacred Scripture is a light for the Church, leading it on to ever greater understanding *(Ibid.*, 6) of God's plan for our salvation.

- *The Creeds and Councils* — The Church has had a long history since the time of Christ. Perhaps in the beginning, an expectation arose in some Christian communities that Jesus would return soon and that the Church would have only a temporary existence. This expectation proved inaccurate. The fullness of revelation was given by our Lord Jesus Christ, but the form of human society has changed dramatically many times since. In all these changes the living Church has tried to proclaim His Gospel clearly in words that each generation could understand. Accurate preservation of the meaning of revelation requires of us a constant reflection and reformulation in order to insure that the truth is adequately transmitted.

Acts 15 records how the apostles in Jerusalem adopted collegial action as a means of guiding the Church in a time of crisis. After the apostolic age, the bishops, like the apostles before them, exercised a collegial responsibility for all the Churches. While each bishop is ordained as a shepherd over the local Church entrusted to his care, he has additional concern for the whole Church in union with his brother bishops. As St. Cyprian noted, "The episcopate is one, of which each bishop holds his part in its totality" (*On the Unity of the Catholic Church* 5).

This collegiality is shown most clearly in the rite of ordination for a bishop, who must be ordained by at least three other bishops. This is a sign that he is in communion with other Churches. The bishop, presiding over the local Church at the eucharistic assembly, realizes the unity of his community with the whole Church through the working of the Holy Spirit.

From the beginning, the episcopate met frequently in local councils to deal with problems and issues that affected more than just the local church. This formed a consciousness within the Church of belonging to the one Church, the one body of Christ without division (Eph 5:4–5). At the beginning of the fourth century, a very serious problem arose that affected the whole Church. Arius, a priest of Alexandria, taught that the Son was subordinate to the Father, thereby undermining the Church's faith in the Trinity. The full divinity of Christ is crucial for the life of a Christian. If Christ is not fully God, union with Christ is not union with God and we are not "partakers of the divine nature" (2 Pt 1:4). In the year 325, a general council was called to consider and deal with this problem. Because it was composed of bishops from all the Churches of the Roman Empire, it was called an "ecumenical" or "universal" synod. In the city of Nicea, 318 bishops met and adopted a creed as the Church's official statement of the faith in response to Arius. This creed or profession of faith defined that Christ was equal to the Father, "Light of Light," and "true God of true God," because He is "of one essence (in Greek, *homoousios*) with the Father." In using the word *homoousios* the Fathers, on the authority given to them by Christ, went beyond the terminology of Sacred Scripture to explain and proclaim for the Church the mystery of Christ. This creed (in the expanded form dating from the Council of Constantinople in 381) has since become the rule of faith for all historic Christian Churches.

The Fathers at the first ecumenical Council did not create the idea of having creeds, nor did they create a profession of faith out of nothing. They considered their task to be the defense of the true faith founded on the continuity of the Church's faith and life. Hence, they turned to the worship of the Church. Formulas of belief were used in the celebration of Holy Baptism, which marks the adoption of persons as children of God and their entrance into the Church. The candidates were asked to make a profession of their faith in the Father and the Son and the Holy Spirit. Their belief about the Trinity was elaborated in formulas that developed in the various local Churches. Such creeds were taught to catechumens on Good Friday as a part of the preparation for their baptism on Holy Saturday. The Council of Nicea apparently accepted the baptismal creed as recited in the Church of Jerusalem as the norm for the whole Church.[3] Later Councils would refer back to this creed as the basic expression of the Church's faith. Thus at the Council of Chalcedon, the Nicene faith was read; and the bishops declared, "This is the faith of all of us: we all so believe."[4] The Creed was also called the "symbol of faith," (i.e. a verbal token of what we believe) or even just "the faith." It was included in the order of the Byzantine Liturgy by Patriarch Timothy of Constantinople about 511.[5]

The core explanations of the Church's basic dogmatic teachings were formulated by the Ecumenical Councils of the first millennium. These councils gathered the bishops of most dioceses of the Eastern Roman Empire together with representatives from the Pope of Rome and other Western dioceses. The teachings of these councils would be accepted or rejected by various local Churches leading to the establishment of various "communions" of these historic Churches.

The Catholic and (Byzantine) Orthodox Churches together recognize seven such councils as ecumenical: 1) Nicea I (325), which defined the divinity of the Son; 2) Constantinople I (381), which defined the divinity of the Holy Spirit; 3) Ephesus (431), which condemned Nestorianism and proclaimed that Christ, truly God, was conceived and born of the Virgin Mary, who may truly be called "God-bearer" (in Greek, *Theotokos*); 4) Chalcedon (451), which accepted the "Tome to Flavian" of St. Leo, Pope of Rome, and defined that Christ was truly God and truly man, one person in two natures; 5) Constantinople II (553), which further explained the definitions of Chalcedon by condemning the "Three Chapters" of Theodore of Mopsuestia and Theodoret and the letter of Ibas to Maris; 6) Constantinople III (680–681), which again further explained Chalcedon by defining that Christ, as true God and true man, has two wills, one divine and one human; and 7) Nicea II (787), which condemned iconoclasm, the opinion that icons of Christ and the saints could not be made.

The Oriental Orthodox Churches (Armenian, Coptic and Syrian) did not accept the fourth council and consequently any that followed. For this reason they are often called "non-

Chalcedonian." The Assyrian Church did not accept Ephesus and so recognizes only the first two councils as ecumenical.

The Byzantine Churches venerate the seven councils during the course of the liturgical year. The first Ecumenical Council, Nicea I, is always commemorated on the Sunday after the feast of the Ascension. The first six Councils are remembered together on the Sunday that falls between July 13–19. The seventh Council is commemorated on the Sunday that falls between October 11–17. The seventh Council has particular importance for the true worship of the Church, for the veneration and use of icons and for its vision that Christ was both God and man and is the image of the Father for us.

The Roman Catholic Church further recognizes fourteen other councils as ecumenical, stipulating that a council is ecumenical when it is so called by the pope. Although none of the early Councils were convened by the pope, his confirmation of their decrees was to be sought.[6] Those councils that particularly involved the Eastern Churches were the following: the Council of Constantinople IV (869–870), which concerned the schism at the time of the Patriarch Photius;[7] the Councils of Lyons (1245) and of Florence (1438–1439), which attempted to make unions with various Orthodox Churches; and the most recent Council, Vatican II, which reaffirmed the importance of ecumenism (the movement to seek the unity of all Christian Churches) and which explicitly recognizes the place and importance of the Eastern Catholic Churches. Representatives of the Eastern Catholic Churches in union with Rome took part at the first and second Vatican Councils (1870, 1962–1965).

- *Fathers of the Church* — The Councils were extraordinary meetings of the bishops, generally called when the Church found itself in a particular crisis. They are an expression of the collegiality of the episcopate. However, individual Christians also have had a formative role in expressing the Tradition. These "Fathers of the Church" are all honored by the Church as witnesses to the tradition of the faith of the Christian people. Most of the Church Fathers were hierarchs, since the specific ministry of a bishop is to be "a light to those in darkness, an instructor of the ignorant, a teacher to the young, a light to the world" (Byzantine prayer at the ordination of bishops). There were also other prominent members of the Christian community who witnessed to the tradition of the faith: priests, deacons, hymnographers, and especially monastics — both men and women — famed for their asceticism and holiness and sought by the faithful for spiritual direction.

The Fathers wrote in a number of forms, the most common being homilies or commentaries, aimed at explaining the Scriptures to the faithful or to the catechumens. St. Cyril of Alexandria, St. Gregory of Nyssa and St. John Chrysostom have left important writings in these forms. Fathers also explained theology for another reason: to provide a defense (in Greek, *apologia*) of the true faith against its detractors both within and from without the Church. Fathers like the second century St. Justin the Philosopher composed apologetic writings to give a true and proper defense of one's actions or beliefs in the still pagan Roman Empire. When the State itself became Christian, "apologies" were still needed to defend the true understandings of the Church against those who introduced false ideas. Thus. St Irenaeus of Lyons opposed the Gnostics, St. Athanasius of Alexandria combatted the Arians, and St. Maximus the Confessor contested the Monothelites.

In addition to commentaries on Scripture and defenses of the faith, many patristic writings were of a specifically spiritual nature, devoted to describing the Christian life and the ways God works in us through the power of the Holy Spirit. They discerned a definite science of the Christian life, which has found concrete expression in the mystical tradition of the Church. Although most ascetical writings were authored by monastics, they assume that every Christian of any station in life is called to perfection in Christ in some way. As St. John

Climacus said, "A Christian is an imitator of Christ in thought, word and deed, as far as this is humanly possible, and believes mightily and blamelessly in the Holy Trinity" (*The Ladder of Divine Ascent* 1).

The Fathers' own prayerful experiences of God and the sometimes severe struggles and sufferings that they endured shine through their works. In this we see that theology, our understanding of God, is very closely bound up with the living of a life in the Spirit. Accurate knowledge of God involves both correct doctrine and authentic religious experience. Living as close as they did to the primitive Christian community, the Fathers' theology included both.

• *The Liturgy* — Another of the principal elements of the Tradition is the Church's divine worship, where liturgical prayers and hymns, which are solidly based on the texts of Scripture and the writings of the Fathers, are proclaimed to and celebrated by a living community. The Eastern Churches have seen the liturgical texts as the work of the Spirit who "makes intercession for us with groanings that cannot be expressed in speech" (Rom 8:26). In fact, when the Fathers wished to articulate the Christian faith, they invariably referred to its expression in the divine services. If a Council were considering whether Christ was truly equal to the Father, the bishops would examine the liturgical prayers to the Father and the Son. Since we worship both equally, our worship proclaims that both the Father and the Son are truly God. This is why, when the First Nicene Council sought a statement of faith, it turned to the baptismal service. In time the Fathers expressed this principle in the saying, "the law of prayer constitutes the law of belief."[8]

Among the most ancient elements of the services are the prayers which address and glorify, God, expressing our relationship with Him. Some hymns actually date from the earliest age of the Church, such as the Vesper hymn, "O Joyful Light." Most of the hymns used today in Byzantine Churches developed after the liturgical prayers. Many were written by monastic poets from the sixth to the tenth centuries. We know the names of most of the hymnographers, both men and women. The greatest of them was St. Romanos the Melodist, sixth century author of many kontakia. His compositions were "sermons in song" that taught much about the faith. Throughout the centuries the troparia, kontakia, stichera and canons of the divine services have been the most important source of theological knowledge for the faithful, especially during times of persecution when other teaching was limited.

• *Theology* — Theology is the Church's expression in ideas and concepts of our relationship with God. The term comes from two Greek words, *theos*, which means "God", and *logos*, which means "word." In its combined form it means the study of God. Theology is not a science like the physical sciences. The latter's task is the objective observation of the material world and the formulation of the laws that govern this world. Authentic theology does not approach God as if He were an object of study. He has revealed Himself as the "Who-Am," the Source of being before whom we bow in worship; and so theology must be approached in the way of the Fathers at the early Councils, "As we pray, so we believe." From the perspective of Byzantine theology, our understanding of God comes from our experience of Him, especially in the mysteries of the Church. From our transformation into this new life, we come to know something of God even though our vision will always be inadequate.

Above all, a theologian must be a person of faith, one who actually achieves union with God through understanding and grace. Anyone who formulates abstract principles about God without experiencing and living them has not really understood them. Theology is not primarily a matter of academic professionalism, but of first-hand knowledge of God. The best way to show the relationship between theology and Christian living is to describe the lives of the three men to whom the Byzantine Church has given the title *"Theologian."*

The first of these was the beloved Apostle and Evangelist John the Theologian. We know only the most basic facts about his life. He was the son of Zebedee and the brother of another apostle, James. Together with Peter, these three formed an inner core even among the twelve apostles. They were present at the raising of the daughter of Jairus (Mk 5:37), at the

Transfiguration (Mt 17:1) and in the garden of Gethsemane (Mt 26:37). John was possibly a young man or even a boy during his discipleship with Jesus. This is just inference from the tradition that he was the last of the apostles to die and was the only one not martyred.

The Gospel of John was the last of the four to be written and is unique because it reflects on the words and deeds of Jesus in a way different from the other Gospels. It proclaims Christ as the eternal Logos, the Word of God, who was manifested in creation and in the experience of Israel. This Gospel expresses in the terminology of Greek philosophy what John personally experienced of God in Jesus Christ: the incarnation of God the Father's love for us (Jn 3:16) and the One who revealed the Holy Spirit. The starting point of Johannine theology can be seen in his first epistle: "This is what we proclaim to you: what was from the beginning, what we have heard, what we have seen with our eyes, what we have looked upon and our hands have touched — we speak of the word of life" (1:1). John saw the same carpenter of Nazareth his contemporaries knew; but his openness to the progressive guidance of the Spirit (cf Jn 16:13) led him to experience the fullness of truth about his Lord.

The second Father to receive the title "Theologian" was St. Gregory of Nazianzus, for a time Archbishop of Constantinople. Gregory was born in the year 330 in Nazianzus where his father later became the bishop. During his university studies, Gregory became a friend of St. Basil the Great. At the age of thirty, he joined St. Basil's monastic community. Shortly afterward on a visit to his hometown, the people seized him and forced him to be ordained a priest. He rebelled at this treatment and ran away, only to return at Pascha and preach an apology for his flight.

Gregory had served his people for about ten years when St. Basil was elected Archbishop of Caesarea in Cappadocia. The Church was experiencing great trials with intense strife between the Orthodox and the Arians. To assist in the struggle, Basil appointed his friend as Bishop of Sasima. Gregory described it as "a detestable little place without water or grass or any mark of civilization." He stayed in Sasima only a short time and returned to Nazianzus to assist and later replace his father. His

mother and his friend, St. Basil, both died soon afterwards.
Gregory then began a new phase in his ministry which would
catapult him to renown in the Church.

The imperial city of Constantinople was in turmoil, divided
between Orthodox Christians and followers of Arius whose
teachings had been condemned fifty-five years earlier in the
Council of Nicea. In the midst of this controversy, St. Gregory
preached five famous homilies on the Holy Trinity, the
Theological Discourses. One historian observed that Gregory,
"in a few pages, and in a few hours, summed up and closed the
controversy of a whole century."9 After only a few months as
Archbishop of Constantinople, further controversies impelled
him to resign from this position which he had not sought and
did not want. He retired to Nazianzus and died there about
eight years later at the age of sixty.10

St. Gregory's theology and his spiritual life were intimately
connected. The Byzantine Church understood this connection
and in later years made his teachings the basis of its own prayer
life. In his first homily as a priest, the apology for his flight after
ordination, Gregory reflected, "Yesterday I was crucified with
[Christ], today I am glorified with Him; yesterday I died with
Him, today I am given life with Him; yesterday I was buried
with Him, today I rise with Him." We pray this text today in the
beautiful Resurrection Canon sung at Matins on Pascha. In the
same way Gregory's *Homily on the Theophany* (No. 38)
became the model for the Byzantine Christmas Canon: "Christ
is born, glorify Him! Christ has come down from heaven, go to
meet Him!"

The third Father to be given the title of theologian was
Simeon, called "the New Theologian" who lived from 949 to
1022. He was born in Galatia in Paphlagonia (Asia Minor) and
his family was part of the local nobility. At the age of 14, he
expressed a desire to enter a monastery, but his spiritual father
had him wait until he was 27. Life in the monastery at that time

was badly in need of reform; and the monks were made uncomfortable by the presence of such a man as Simeon, who was zealous to lead a life of Christian perfection. He was dismissed from the Studite monastery, the most famous in Constantinople, but was quickly accepted in the small monastery of St. Mammas. In only three years, he was elected hegumen, a post he held for twenty-five years. Simeon vigorously pursued the reform of the monastery, but was constantly opposed by some of his monks and by the Emperor's theologian, the Archbishop Stephen. Finally in the year 1009, he was removed from his post and exiled into a small village named Paloukiton. Here he established a small monastery with those disciples who followed him into exile. He remained there to his death thirteen years later even though the Patriarch Sergius lifted his exile and offered to ordain him an Archbishop.[11]

St. Simeon was the first Byzantine mystic to speak so freely about his own spiritual experiences. He emphasized the importance of a personal experience of Christ, and he was zealous for an authentic spiritual life and Christian perfection. Simeon saw the connection between the Scriptures, the theology of the Greek Fathers, such as St. Gregory the Theologian, and the writings of ascetic Fathers like St. John Climacus. More importantly, like the other "Theologians," Simeon spoke on the basis of a deeply personal experience of God. Simeon describes this — in the third person — as an experience of God as light:

"One day, as he stood and recited, 'God, have mercy on me, a sinner,' uttering it with his mind rather than his mouth, suddenly a flood of divine radiance appeared from above and filled all the room. As it happened the young man lost all awareness of his surroundings and forgot that he was in a house or that he was under a roof. He saw nothing but light all around him and did not know whether he was standing on the ground.... . Instead, he was wholly in the presence of immaterial light and seemed to himself to have turned into light. Oblivious of all the world he was filled with tears and with ineffable joy and gladness."[12]

St John the Theologian had taught that "God is light ; in Him there is no darkness at all" (1 Jn 1:5; cf also Jn 8:12). Simeon witnessed in his own life to a conscious experience of this divine Light and proclaimed that every believer could have the same.

AUTHORITY AND HOLINESS

One of the gifts which the Church receives from the Spirit is the charism of authority. Our English words "author" and "authority" come from the Latin *auctor* and *auctoritas*. They refer to the quality of being an author: to develop, to make decisions, to increase. Jesus the Lord, remains the Church's true authority, because He alone is the author of our salvation. However He gave the apostles a share in His authority, which was to be accepted as His own (cf Lk 10:16). As the eyewitnesses of His resurrection, the apostles transmitted from personal knowledge the message of Jesus. They were the first preachers of Christ's Gospel and retain a specal place in the Church for all time. Their mission was beautifully described in 1 Jn 1:1, noted above. The authoritative role exercised by the apostles is recorded in the Acts of the Apostles and in the Letters written by them, especially by St. Paul. Among the apostles St. Peter had a special role as seen by his intervention at the Council in Jerusalem (Acts 15:7–12).

The authority of these eyewitnesses was unique; after their repose, a similar kind of authority in the Church was exercised by its overseers, the bishops *(episcopos* in Greek, literally "overseer"). Writing at the beginning of the second century, St. Ignatius of Antioch was one of the first Fathers to witness to the bishop's authority. He wrote to the Ephesians, "It is manifest, therefore, that we should look upon the bishop even as we would look upon the Lord himself" (*Ephesians* 6). The *Apostolic Constitutions* (2.33.3) tell us that the bishops inherited the power of binding and loosing that was given to the apostles. The ordination prayers of the Byzantine Church calls the bishop an "apostle, prophet and teacher ... (and) the follower of (the Lord), the true shepherd who gave his life for his sheep." Thus, the Church still exercises the charism of authority given to it by Christ through the Holy Spirit.

The gifts of organization and structure are essential to the Church. They enable it to pass on the Gospel of our Lord and to continue to proclaim it to various peoples at different times of history. Not surprisingly in the course of the Church's history, Christians in leadership positions have made many errors of judgement. Yet in all this, the Church has never lacked for people through whom the Holy Spirit has worked through another of His gifts: the charism of holiness. In each age heroes of faith and charity have emerged to serve as beacons for others. They have taught the way to truth and goodness consistently, enabling us to profess belief in "one, *holy*, catholic and apostolic Church."

THE THEOTOKOS, TYPE OF THE CHURCH

The Church as Body of Christ and Temple of the Holy Spirit is exemplified by the Holy Virgin, who was the actual physical vessel containing Christ. She whom the Byzantine Churches call the "living temple of the holy glory of Christ our God," "the holy temple of our holy God," and "the sublime Temple, the palace, throne and wondrous abode of our God" (Stichera at Vespers, Feast of the Entrance into the Temple) is the model or "type" of the people of God, who have become His dwelling place (1 Cor 3:16-17; 6:19; 2 Cor 6:16).

The Virgin's receptivity to God is revealed particularly in the story of the Annunciation (Lk 1:26-38). The angel Gabriel appeared to her with the astonishing news that she would be the virgin mother of the Son of the Most High, through the power of the Spirit. Mary freely chose, without hesitation, to cooperate with God's will and His plan for our salvation. Her response anticipated the petition of our Lord, "Thy will be done, on earth as it is in heaven." This complete assent to God's will, without conditions, is the very essence of sanctity: the complete and open acceptance of our human destiny, the end for which we were created.

Eve's refusal to follow God's plan in Eden brought only death and suffering. By her openness to God's design, Mary heralds the New Creation in Christ. She is the first to be saved through the death and resurrection of her Son. In her dormition ("falling asleep"), human nature is raised to the plane of the angelic powers. The Psalmist praised God who "made [man] little less than the angels, and crowned him with glory and honor," but Mary represents a new creation. She is "higher in honor than the Cherubim and beyond compare more glorious than the Seraphim." She thereby becomes the model of sanctity for all who seek Christian perfection, especially the ascetics or "God-bearers" whom the Church describes as "angels in the body."

Byzantine theology is even clearer about Mary's role in the salvation of the human race. On the feast of the Annunciation, Gabriel is described as greeting Mary as the one "through whom Adam is called back to Paradise, Eve is freed from bondage, and the world is filled with joy." In her womb, God is united with human flesh "through the good will of the Father and the operation of the Holy Spirit" (Liti Stichera). On the feast of the Dormition, the Church proclaims, "Rejoice, O Virgin, for you alone brought heaven and earth together in giving birth to your Son" (Stichera at the Praises), and "through her holy Dormition the world is given new life" (Liti Stichera). As the one who gave birth to God in the flesh, Mary's choices had cosmic significance; and she is the first to participate in the complete salvation wrought through the incarnation of Christ, including the assumption of her body into the presence of God. Thus she has a unique role as intercessor for all humanity. One of the most ancient prayers of the Church describes her role, "We hasten to your patronage, O Virgin Mother of God. Despise not our prayers in our necessities, but deliver us from all danger, you who alone are pure and blessed." Byzantine Church history contains many examples of prayer vigils to the Theotokos in times of civil danger. One such occasion gave rise to the feast of the Protection of the Mother of God (October 1).

Scripture honors Mary with most beautiful names: "highly favored one" (Lk 1:28), "blessed among women" (1:28,42), and "mother of the Lord" (1:43). These became the basis for all the titles ascribed to the Holy Virgin. The greatest title given to Mary is that of *Theotokos*, Greek for "she who bore God." It was given to her by the Council of Ephesus (431) which defined that "Emmanuel is truly God, and therefore the Holy Virgin is the Theotokos, inasmuch as in the flesh [in her womb] she bore the Word of God made flesh" (Canon 1). This Council very clearly rejected all opinions about the personality of Jesus that would in any way separate the divine and human natures united in Him. It refused any implication that the divinity was united to Him after His birth or that Jesus is in any way distinguished from the Word of God. Mary was not simply the mother of Jesus the man, but of Jesus the incarnate Son of God. Both natures were united in His person. Through her relationship to this one person, she is the "Mother of God." The Byzantine Churches ordinarily refer to Mary by this title of Theotokos, which signifies that she is truly the "Mother of God" through her conception, bearing, and giving birth to the person Jesus, true God and true man.

Epilogue

The history of the Church is really the story of people who are responding to God's call to live in His kingdom. Each of us has our personal story, the ongoing saga of life. Some people are more aware of their stories and of God's presence in their lives. Others have only a vague or generalized sense of God's presence with them. The difference is in our ability to reflect on our experiences in life.

Experience means more than simply doing something or having something happen to us. Repeating an act for twenty years does not necessarily mean that we have twenty years of experience. We may not learn anything from routine repetition. Experience comes through *reflection*. We must reflect on this event for it to lead to experience. Simply living each day without reflection on events is mere existence. Some go on putting one foot in front of the other without knowing where they are going or why they are going there. Life must be more than plain existence. Real life is living each day with all that day brings, pausing to reflect on this experience, noting the events that happen to us as a result of our choices, and deciding whether or not these choices accurately reflect our values and principles. Then do we rise above mere existence to really living.

God calls us to be truly alive, to be in a conscious relationship with the persons of the Trinity. This relationship can occur only when we come to know both ourselves and the persons of the Trinity: Father, Son and Holy Spirit. This means that each day we must take some time to look back over the day and note what has happened. We see both the happy events and the more burdensome ones. We see some as life-giving and others as missed opportunities to enter into life. Occasionally certain events take on

95

meaning only in such a time of reflection. Without this time they would have simply fallen into oblivion, and their lessons would have been lost to us forever.

Through such reflection, we begin to see ourselves in a clearer light. Certain patterns of behavior as well as certain presuppositions and even prejudices may emerge. Simply put, we learn much about ourselves. Further reflection enables us to visualize our patterns of behavior and gain insight into why we react in certain ways. We may recognize some of our motives and reasons for acting as we do, and change accordingly. All of this is needed for growth and for life.

Such patterns of reflection go beyond teaching us about ourselves to reveal the presence of God in our lives. A careful review of our daily activity will bring to mind the ways we have responded to the persons and events that touched us. We can then begin to note the times when we were responding to God's call to life. How did I respond to this call? Was I aware of God's presence? Perhaps we become consciously aware of this presence only in this time of reflection.

THE CALL TO FAITH: MY PERSONAL HISTORY

These times of reflection on my own behavior and on God's presence can allow me to see my life as more than a series of disconnected events. As we become aware of the aspects of our own personality, we see ourselves as affected by our relationships with others, the society or culture in which we live, the media, the environment and a host of other factors. Our reflections may lead us to discover more than our responses and the patterns of the world around us. We may see that regardless of circumstances or of our response, God is constantly with us at all times and in all ways, even in times when we were not thinking about Him. We come to know God's presence underlying our total existence. He is always there with us.

Ancient Israel made this discovery. After wandering through the desert without knowing where they were going or what they were doing, they finally settled in the Promised Land. They had a chance to reflect on their journey, their history and their story. Through this reflection they came to see the hand of God continually guiding them, even in their unfaithfulness. God's presence did not depend on their response or their goodness. It was a gift freely given and beyond all merit. They reflected further on the mystery of their existence, the purpose of their lives, how they came to be, why they experienced different pulls in their lives, why both good and evil exist, and where all things come from.

The first chapters of Genesis give us the fruits of their reflections. They saw that God had created everything as good and had blessed it all. He had created us in His very image and likeness to share a special relationship with Him. Yet at times, we humans choose to go our own way, to turn from God's plan for us, to choose death and not life. God, however, does not abandon us even in our turning away from Him:

> And yet, O gracious Lord, You did not turn away from Your creation, nor did You forget the work of Your hands, but You visited us in various ways because of Your merciful loving-kindness: You sent prophets and wrought mighty works through the saints, who in every generation have been pleasing to You. You spoke to us through Your servants, the prophets, who foretold to us the salvation that was to come. You gave the law as an aid, and appointed angels as our guardians, and when the fullness of time had come, You spoke to us through Your Son Himself (Anaphora, Liturgy of St. Basil).

The Scriptural account of the creation and fall, of essential goodness and inherent weakness, is the story of each of us. What seems to be most unique and intimate to us reveals itself to be the most universal. The story of the People of God is also the story of each of His people. Salvation history is also my history. As I reflect on this, I can see how my story of my own relationship to God conforms to the larger story of God's people. Thus I can interpret my own story in the light of the Scriptures; they become my guide for my personal journey.

Our insight into our personal history and motives, together with holy examples from salvation history, and especially our sacramental incorporation into Christ help us to understand our lives. Viewing reality through faith's eyes inserts my story into salvation history and helps me to interpret my own relationship with God. However, we cannot rest secure in this inner world; we must also live and act amid society. We are called to live truly according to Christian values, a formidable task in a society that welcomes mediocrity, fears principles, and exalts egotistical and selfish ways. A reflective life, lived in faith, fully in union with the Trinity, is indeed a witness to the world around us. As Christians, we will always be people "not of this age." If our lives are not challenging the mediocrity around us, then perhaps our light is not shining as brightly as it should. We are permitting it to be hidden under bushel baskets.

A life of witness is never easy. To be a challenge to others and to be constantly challenged ourselves requires great inner strength. It also requires a great deal of humility and honesty. Thus we are called to a life of continual conversion, "to spend the rest of our lives in peace and repentance." To accept this daunting challenge, we need to know that we are loved and accepted by God and that we are sinners. We need to remember that we have been raised up to new life in Christ and filled with His Holy Spirit who lives and breathes in us. The awesomeness of this realization calls forth a deep awareness of our unworthiness of such a gift and a true humility before God. At the same time, it challenges us to be a witness for the faith.

The martyrs and confessors for the faith are the true witnesses and guides. In them the sense of God's presence was nurtured until it grew so strong that it could not be denied. It shone forth in their words and actions. Even though they suffered and many were put to death, their witness continued to speak even after death. Their strength came not from themselves or their own innate goodness, but from their awareness of their weakness and sinfulness which required them to turn daily to God for His aid. It came from their powerful awareness of His dynamic presence in their lives, impelling them to act and to have a lasting impact on the culture and the society around them. My personal faith must never stay locked up in an inner world. Rather, I must respond to its challenge to live and to call others to image God's presence in the world. My faith pervades my life and calls me to an ever deeper fidelity.

Notes

PROLOGUE

1. Raymond Brown et al, eds. *The Jerome Biblical Commentary* (Englewood Cliffs, NJ: Prentice Hall, 1968) s.v. John L. McKenzie, "The Gospel According to St. Matthew."

CHAPTER ONE: THE MYSTERY OF GOD

1. Gregory of Nyssa, *Commentary on Ecclesiastes* 7, in Kenneth Leech, *Experiencing God* (San Francisco: Harper and Row, 1985), 160.
2. John Chrysostom, *The Incomprehensibility of God* 3, in Leech, *God*, 165.
3. Maximus the Confessor, *Two Hundred Texts on Theology*, in *The Philokalia*, Vol. 2, trans. G.E.H. Palmer, P. Sharrard and K. Ware (London and Boston: Faber and Faber, 1981), 114.
4. Gregory of Nyssa, *The Life of Moses*, in Herbert Musurillo, *From Glory to Glory* (Crestwood, NY: St. Vladimir's Seminary Press, 1979), 44.
5. Gregory of Nyssa, *Commentary on the Song of Songs* 11, in Leech, *God*, 169.
6. Pseudo-Dionysius, *The Ecclesiastical Hierarchy*, 3.1
7. *Divine Liturgy of St. John Chrysostom*, Prayer Before the "Our Father".
8. *Divine Liturgy of St. Basil the Great*, Prayer at the Consumption of the Holy Gifts.

CHAPTER TWO: THE MYSTERY REVEALED

1. M. Scott Peck, *People of the Lie* (New York: Simon and Schuster, 1983), 207.
2. Gregory the Theologian, *Sermon on Holy Baptism* 7, in *Baptism*, ed. Andre Hamman (Staten Island, N.Y.: Alba House, 1967), 91-92.

3.   John Chrysostom, Homily 25 on John, cited in *Ancient Christian Writers, vol. 31*

4.   John Chrysostom, Homily 6 on Colossians, cited in *Ancient Christian Writers, vol. 31*

5.   Maximos the Confessor, *Mystagogy* 21, trans. George Berthold (New York: Paulist Press, 1985), 203.

6.   Harry Merwyn Buck, Jr., "The Johannine Lectionary," in *Studies in the Lectionary Text of the Greek New Testament* 2.4 (Chicago: University of Chicago Press, 1958), 1–2.

7.   John Damascene, *Exposition of the Orthodox Faith*, in *Post-Nicene Fathers* (reprint, Grand Rapids, Mich.: Eerdmans, 1973), Vol. 2, 69. Perhaps the kingdom is Christ Himself, and our entrance into the kingdom is our union with Christ. St. Paul reasons that the Christian mystery is "Christ in you, your hope of glory" (Col 1:27). This reality is reflected in the Byzantine liturgical greeting, "Christ is among us! He is and will be!"

8.   Simeon the New Theologian, "Discourse 6.4," trans. C. J. deCatanzaro in *Symeon the New Theologian: The Discourses*. (New York: Paulist Press, 1980), 122.

9.   Nicholas Cabasilas, *The Life in Christ*, 1.3, trans. Carmino J. deCatanzaro (Crestwood, N.Y.: St. Vladimir's Seminary Press, 1974), 1.1, 43.

10.   The place of failure is called "hell." It should not be confused with *"Hades"* (Greek for the Hebrew *"Sheol"*) as the place of shadow for detention of departed souls awaiting the resurrection of Christ. This is the "hell" referred to in the Apostles' Creed, "[Christ] descended into hell." By contrast no hope exists in the place of eternal condemnation. This hell is the translation of the Hebrew Gehenna, the Valley of Hennom, which served as the garbage dump of Jerusalem and burned continually.

11.   John Damascene, *Exposition of the Orthodox Faith* 4.9, op. cit, 79.

12.   The basic concept of the purification of souls after death is based on 2 Maccabees 12:39–45 and 1 Corinthians 3:11–15. The need for purification was taught by several Fathers of East and West (among the earliest: St. Clement of Alexandria, *Stromata* 7.6). The Western Church, after St. Augustine (*City of God*, 21.13, 24), elaborated this concept in the doctrine of "purgatory", a place of painful purification, which was

defined at the Councils of Lyons and Florence, which were called to ratify unions with the Byzantine Church. The Council of Trent reaffirmed these definitions, but forbade fantastic descriptions. The Eastern Churches have been reluctant to speak with assurance of a separate place of purification or to describe that purification as "painful". Yet none have been more committed to prayer that the departed be granted rest with the saints. In any dialogue on this question, Roman Catholics must admit that the description of purgatory was influenced by medieval mythology.

CHAPTER THREE - THE MYSTERY SHARED

1. Maximos the Confessor, *Mystagogy*, 187-188.

2. John Meyendorff, *Living Tradition* (Crestwood, N.Y.: St. Vladimir's Seminary Press, 1978), 21.

3. J. N. D. Kelly, *Early Christian Creeds* (New York: David McKay Co., Inc., 1972), 227.

4. Acts of the Council of Chalcedon, in *Post-Nicene Fathers*, Vol. 14, 249.

5. Robert Taft, *The Great Entrance* (Rome: Orientalia Christiana Analecta 200, 1975), 399.

6. Wilhelm de Vries, *Orient et Occident* (Paris: Les Editions du Cerf, 1974).

7. cf. Francis Dvornik, *The Photian Schism, History and Legend* (1948, 1970, Cambridge: Cambridge University Press).

8. "Lex supplicandi legem statuat credendi." This Western maxim is especially applicable to the Eastern Church, where the liturgical life is so much the center of faith and community. For an explanation of this principle, read Aidan Kavanagh, *On Liturgical Theology* (New York: Pueblo Publishing Co., 1974). See also John Meyendorff, *Byzantine Theology* (New York: Fordham University Press, 1974), 115–125.

9. De Broglie, *L'Eglise et L'Empire*, p. 385, quoted in *Post-Nicene Fathers*, Vol. 7, 280.

10. Payne, *Holy Fire*, 170–194.

11. cf. deCatanzaro, *Symeon the New Theologian*, 1–12.

12. *Ibid.*, 7.

Glossary of Liturgical and Theological Terms

ANAPHORA — The great Eucharistic Prayer, the heart of the Divine Liturgy, beginning with the invocation "Let us give thanks to the Lord" and concluding with the prayers of intercession.

APOPHATIC THEOLOGY — The teaching of the Eastern Fathers that human thought can only reflect on God's essence using negative language, describing what God is not, since this divine essence is unknowable *(see pp 11-13).*

ARIANISM — The doctrine that the Logos or Word of God was created by the Father. It was condemned in 325 AD by the First Ecumenical Council which taught that the Word is "of one essence with the Father" (Nicene Creed).

CANON — A poetical composition of nine odes, each made up of several troparia, which is sung at matins and certain other services. The theme of each ode is taken from a corresponding biblical canticle.

DEISIS — Literally, "prayer". An icon of Christ, usually enthroned, surrounded by saints and angels who are shown facing Him with their hands raised in prayer. The figures closest to Christ are usually the Theotokos and St. John the Forerunner.

DIVINE LITURGY — The principal term for the Eucharistic service in Byzantine Churches. The **Liturgy of St. Basil the Great**, used on the Sundays of the Great Fast and on a few other days, now differs only in its principal prayers from the **Liturgy of St. John Chrysostom** which is used the rest of the year. The **Presanctified Liturgy**, served on Lenten weekdays, is not a full Liturgy, but Vespers, followed by the distribution of Communion.

GNOSTICISM — A variety of religious movements, flourishing in the Roman Empire during the first five centuries AD, which stressed some secret teachings available only to those who have been initiated into them. Many tried to synthesize such systems with Christianity.

GREAT FAST (GREAT LENT) — The 40-day fast period preceeding Great Week and the celebration. It is called "great" to distinguish it from the less austere and shorter fasts before the feasts of Christmas, Ss. Peter and Paul, and the Dormition of the Theotokos.

GREAT HOURS (ROYAL HOURS) — An expanded form of the daily services (First, Third, Sixth, and Ninth Hours) used on the vigils of Christmas and the Throphany and on Great Friday. They are sometimes called "Royal" because the Byzantine emperor was accustomed to attending them in state.

GREAT (AND HOLY) WEEK — The week preceeding Pascha, each day of which commemorates one or more events of the death and resurrection of Christ.

KONTAKION — A form of liturgical hymn consisting of alternating troparia and verses (also called Akathist). The kontakia used in most Byzantine services today are, or are based on, the first troparion of the more ancient and longer hymns.

LAMB (EUCHARISTIC) — The portion of the holy bread which is cut from the loaf during the rite of preparation and consecrated at the Divine Liturgy.

LITI — Literally, "entreaty". A procession with hymns and a litany of intercession added to Vespers on the eves of the Great Feasts.

MATINS (ORTHROS) — The dawn or morning service, consisting of psalms, hymns, biblical canticles and litanies. On Sundays and greater feasts the reading and veneration of the Gospel is added.

MONOTHELITISM — The teaching that Christ, although of two natures, had only one will. It was first proposed by Patriarch Sergius of Constantinople in 638 AD and condemned at Constantinople III in 681 as contradicting the true humanity of Christ.

MYSTERIES — The Eastern term for sacraments, referring to the hidden power of God working in them.

SEPTUAGINT — The Greek version of the Old Testament, incorporating translations of the Hebrew books as well as the inclusion of others. Usually designated **LXX**, the Septuagint is the normative version of the Old Testament in the Byzantine Churches.

STICHERON — A Byzantine liturgical chant, usually longer than a troparion, found in vespers, matins and certain other services.

SYMBOL OF FAITH — From the word for "sign of recognition". It refers to the Creed, which is meant to be a sign by which we recognize our common faith.

SYNAXIS — Literally, "assembly", usually for worship. It usually refers to the second day of a Feast, when there is another celebration to honor a secondary figure associated with the feast. It may also refer to the Divine Liturgy, especially the section preceeding the little entrance.

SYNOPTICS — The closely related Gospels of Ss. Matthew, Mark and Luke. All three have a similar basic arrangement of events, and even of details in contrast to St. John's Gospel. Modern commentators have seen various kinds of interdependence among the three.

TABLE OF PREPARATION — The table at the north side of the altar area where the holy gifts are prepared prior to the Divine Liturgy. It is usually situated in a niche or separate chapel.

THEOPHANY — Literally, "the manifestation of God". Title of the January 6 feast celebrating the manifestation of the Trinity at the occasion of Christ's baptism in the Jordan.

TROPARION — A brief liturgical chant, usually referring to the theme of the feast celebrated.

VESPERS — The evening service, consisting of psalms, hymns, biblical canticles and litanies. On Saturdays and greater feasts Old Testament readings are added.

Index of Scripture References and Citations

Old Testament

Index of Patristic Citations